The Sailing Chef

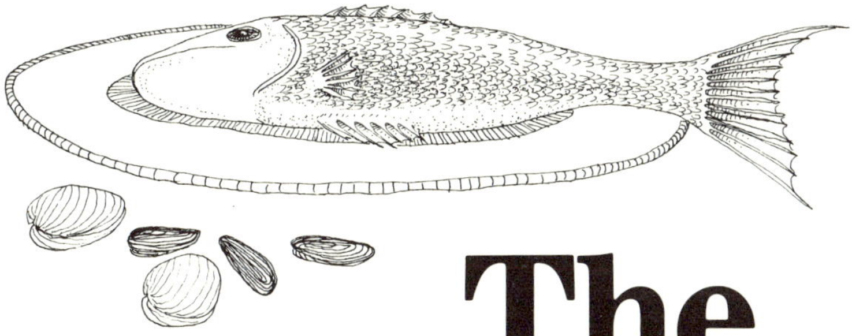

The Sailing Chef

TY HARRINGTON

Photographs by the author

Drawings by Michael R. Brennecke

Walker and Company

NEW YORK

The author gratefully acknowledges the help of John Loeper, Mary-Beth Sweetland Quinn, Nancy Watson, Karl Harr, Skip Hull, Budd Gray, Lori Mainelli, Gerry, Don and Jeff.

First published in the United States of America in 1978 by the Walker Publishing Company, Inc.

Published simultaneously in Canada by Beaverbooks, Limited, Pickering, Ontario.

ISBN: 0-8027-0582-0

Library of Congress Catalog Card Number: 77-80358

Printed in the United States of America

10 9 8 7 6 5 4 3 2 1

To My Grandparents

CONTENTS

ACKNOWLEDGMENTS

PART ONE
The Steward's Handbook 1

One	Some Thoughts on Cooking at Sea	3
Two	The Galley—Like No Kitchen on Earth	9
Three	Keeping Your Cool	27
Four	Jury-Rigging: Tips and Tricks for Making Do	33
Five	Cooking Up a Storm	37
Six	Any Port in a Storm	41
Seven	Practical Provisioning	45
Eight	Safety at Sea	55

PART TWO
The Steward's Recipes 61

Nine	Breakfast	63
Ten	Lunch	75
Eleven	Dinner	89
Twelve	Vegetables, Salads and Sauces	109
Thirteen	Dessert	121
Fourteen	Fondue	127
Fifteen	Snacks	131
Sixteen	Meals for Stormy Weather	133

APPENDIX: A TABLE OF SUBSTITUTIONS 141
INDEX 143

PART ONE The Steward's Handbook

Chapter One

SOME THOUGHTS ON COOKING AT SEA

All you want is a cup of coffee, but there's not a match on the entire boat. A minor problem? I've watched seasoned sailors scour their vessels from stem to stern, and virtually offer Neptune their right arm if only he would provide a match.

A few more deprivations like this and you can return from even a mere eight hours on the water feeling as if you've endured all the hardships of primitive living in a single day. Yet in less time than it takes to ransack the boat, you can take steps that will return you to port as comfortable as if you had spent the day ashore.

How do you solve the problems involved in cooking at sea? What can you do to create simple, yet interesting and nourishing meals instead of an endless diet of canned beef stews and dehydrated glop? To get the answers, I interviewed dozens of sea cooks, adding their knowledge to my own. As a result, no matter how you travel—by sail or by engine, by day, week or year—this book will give you the benefit of hundred of years of combined experience in the galley.

The first part of the book deals with the mechanics of cooking afloat. Except that both prepare food, there are few similarities between a cook ashore and one in the galley. Even the cookingest landlubber never has to contend with a stove that rolls port to starboard, or a refrigerator (icebox, more likely) which should only be opened three times a day. When you leave land, even the shape of your day changes; menus and mealtimes must conform.

Once offshore, clocks get cast aside and sunrise signals the start of most days. Usually you have weighed anchor and are making headway even before your eyes are fully open. Breakfast is a real meal, not just a few bites gulped down in time to catch the bus. It must be nutritious, filling enough to last until lunch, but not too heavy. And it should be simple enough to be prepared quickly and sleepily.

Lunch, routine enough at home, is the trickiest meal on a boat. It can rarely be planned very far in advance. On the water weather changes very quickly. What begins as a warm weekend can easily end with blowing rain, in spite of the weather forecast. As the weather comes 'round, so must your luncheon menu. Chef's Salad may be what you had in mind, but if it gets blustery and damp, you'll have to switch resourcefully to a hot meal and stow the salad for a fair day.

Again, if the seas get really rough, you have to set a galley storm sail, making a meal that will be ready and hot all afternoon to accommodate the busy crew, with each member eating at a different time. It must also warm chilled bodies and be as intestinally pacifying as possible.

The end of the day also follows the sun. Unless you have better-than-average galley lighting, you'll want dinner served almost as soon as you drop the hook. This means fixing the day's largest meal while still underway, without subjecting yourself to undue time below measuring spoonfuls and checking directions, a task to try even the ancient mariner's cast-iron stomach. If you spend more than an hour fixing dinner, not only will your stomach feel the strain, you may be keelhauled by shipmates who are in a ravenous state after hours of sniffing enticing odors.

Despite these and other problems, like the ever-present threat of unexpected guests and suddenly burgeoning appetites, dinner can be your most creative meal, without an entire afternoon of prep work, without an oven, and without help. Just to be inventive, experiment with a hibachi and an oriental cooking wok, and don't try to pretend that your galley is simply a floating kitchen.

In short, cooking afloat is unique. If you're an experienced hand in the kitchen, do your best to forget what you already know the minute you step aboard. If it's all new to you, don't despair; many of the best ocean cooks I've met have been novices—unhampered by prior experience, their imaginative jury-rigging in the galley consistently creates extremely seaworthy concoctions.

The essence of successful cooking at sea is simplicity; use the absolute minimum necessary to produce maximum results. Each item must be selected for a good reason. Every utensil, every pot and every pan must serve more than one purpose or it wastes space—a class-A felony on any boat regardless of size. All food should be filled to the brim with food value. There is absolutely no room for empty calories. This does not mean that meals need be spartan, nor the cook a wizard. It does, however, require extra planning and careful attention to details that could pass safely unheeded ashore.

Snacks, for example, not only need to please, they should also supply some basic food value, augment nutrition, replace fluids drained by the sun, even make up for a missed breakfast. Snacks should also be able to stand alone, as a meal for unexpected guests or even as emergency food.

However, the shipboard notion of simplicity may be confusing. Often what is quite simple in a landlocked kitchen is unworkable at sea. Prepackaged meals, for instance, are time-savers for the home, but bulky on a boat and usually more work than starting from scratch. In addition, processing reduces food value. "Easy-to-follow" package recipes often require additional ingredients, present in every home, but easily overlooked in provisioning a boat. Packaged meals often have a taste-alike dullness when relied upon as a staple food.

Whenever possible, I recommend using fresh meats and produce. Though they require a little more planning, basic fresh foods provide the greatest food value. They are extremely versatile and adaptable to a greater variety of dishes. Onions, eggs and potatoes, the basic staples carried by 'round-the-world sailor and gourmet Sir Francis Chichester, bear this out. All three will keep for at least ten days without refrigeration; yes, even eggs seem to stand up very well, especially if kept beneath the water line in the hold. All three have good food value. And all lend themselves to myriad recipes, preparations so diverse that they may be served in successive meals without one bearing a boring resemblance to the other. Incidentally, fresh foods also tend to be far less expensive than processed foods.

Successful cooking at sea depends on developing the ability

to anticipate problems before they arise. Try to think in terms of motion, of cramped accommodations (no one wants his bedroom, which doubles as the living and dining room, to smell all night of garlic, or worse, burned chicken broth). Once you adjust your thinking to this new genre, cooking on a boat becomes quite logical.

If you are already used to cooking under away-from-home conditions, or are receiving advice from an outdoor-loving friend, beware of a common trap. Many mistakenly equate cooking afloat with camping or other methods of cooking on the move. Again, I repeat, boating, from a cook's angle at least, is unique. For example, it is true that a broad, flat frying pan will serve as a cook-all-quickly on a camping trip because of its large surface area. But, on a boat, if the pan has shallow sides, the dinner is far more likely to wind up on the deck (or on you) than on the table. Better to use a wide-bottomed pot that has high sides and a top. If the pot is of good quality—and since you don't have to carry it in your backpack, a little extra weight is not a problem—it will be possible to cook just as quickly in it as in a frying pan. By filling it only half or quarter full, you can leave it alone if properly secured, on the stove without fear that it won't be there when you return.

Grease, another item fairly easy to cope with in the woods, can be the bane of a sea cook's day. In addition to being generally messy to handle, grease aboard a ship is downright dangerous. If it spills, it can easily catch on fire, and dousing it with water can cause an explosion. It's slippery and can't be easily cleaned up. Grease will clog drains, requiring a complete overhaul because plastic piping prevents use of chemical drain openers. Also, fatty foods are generally less good for you, and especially unwelcome at sea. With a little forethought you can avoid these hassles. For instance, when purchasing meat, buy it lean, or have the extra fat trimmed off.

Of course, regardless of how much of a boating frame of mind you're in, and no matter how thoroughly you plan ahead, there are bound to be situations you will learn to deal with only through experience. I once planned a fairly elaborate dinner that I was certain I could prepare inside half an hour, using a hibachi to augment my two-burner stove. In no time meat and potatoes were roasting away on the hibachi, hung over the stern. The crew was below changing out of swim suits after a dip; I

was in the galley tending to the stove. In twenty-five minutes everything was all set to go. I just had to grab the food off the hibachi and serve. So I climbed topside to the hibachi—the meat and potatoes were gone! A still-hovering flock of gulls had deftly snatched everything, including my spatula, and we dined a bit later than expected. Which shows that no matter how carefully you plan, there won't be many dull moments. Now I have not only rigged up several contraptions to keep the gulls off, I also keep a camera handy in the galley to record such scenes, which after the trip often become the hilarious highlights. A sense of humor is one of the best sanity-saving devices aboard.

In the following pages I have tried to give you the benefit of the mistakes made by myself and the hundreds of boaters I have interviewed. A mistake may be a positive learning experience the first time, but there is no reason why every boater has to start from scratch.

Above all, cookery at sea should be enjoyable and satisfying; I have tried to tailor this book to that end. I cannot eliminate all work, but I have tried to direct your efforts toward meaningful results, and to make your boating a pleasure instead of an ordeal. I hope you will come to think of cooking aboard a boat as a unique and valuable skill.

Though on land you may often feel unappreciated, once on the water you are the only game going, and as the nearest restaurant will be a wet walk away, you are in a strong position to demand recognition!

Along with captains and navigators, skilled sea cooks have traditionally enjoyed positions of respect. Though they no longer double as ship's doctor, they are still largely responsible for the basic health and well-being of all aboard. Along the New England coast, where I cooked aboard a topsail schooner, it is common practice for the cook to enjoy the rank and status of an officer—high pay, a choice of berths, and relieved of standing all watches.

If you master your craft, your good tasty food can easily become the highlight of the long days on the water. Though you may get neither high pay nor choice of berths, you will be as important as the motor or the mast to the success of any voyage—be it a day, a weekend or a year.

Chapter Two

THE GALLEY—LIKE NO KITCHEN ON EARTH

Autumn on Buzzards Bay: southwest winds held steady at thirty knots. Ploughing competitively towards Woods Hole, the two schooners sailed so closely abeam the captains navigated by each others' binnacles. Below, in the galley of the *Bill of Rights*, I ran another race—turkey with all the trimmings and four vegetables for forty.

Catching a gust, we dipped another five degrees and, scuppers awash, slid into the lead. Suddenly there was an unexpected thunderclap and the strained threads of the mains' exploded apart. Without leaving my station at the galley's water pump, I knew the win was *Shenandoah*'s.

No sooner had the uproar above me calmed than the next moment of panic was mine. Without warning the reassuring roar of the Shipmate stove's sunrise-to-sunset diesel-fueled fire died and the galley, except for my long moan, was quiet.

I exhausted dinner's fifteen-minute margin in discovering the clogged fuel-line problem, then covered with soot, climbed on deck to add notice of a cold dinner to the captain's other concerns. Back in the galley I punted with leftovers, and after a frantic half hour a Chef's Salad dinner emerged, with none but the captain and the mate the wiser. While all ate, I unclogged the fuel line, and there was roast turkey for lunch the next day.

Though sails do not blow out nor stoves die everyday, at sea these occasions are constantly in the wings waiting to happen. Just as deck hands always have needle and thread ready to turn palms-up and sew sail, the cook needs resources so that a thing like a dead stove does not mean all aboard go without a decent meal.

Versatility and simplicity are the watchwords of cooking at sea. Behind every good ocean cook stands a well-ordered galley which reflects the needs of the vessel it serves.

The Location of the Galley—Some Problems May Already Be Built In

Every aspect of every boat is based on compromise. Comfort gives way to a faster hull, the convenience of electricity adds complications of a generator, and no matter where the galley is placed, disadvantages appear. Bearing this in mind, the trick is to note a galley's shortcomings and compensate whenever possible.

In bygone days, when pleasure craft were fewer and most small vessels were workboats, galleys were placed forward to maximize cargo area and work space aft. The cook, rolling about in a low forward compartment, had to manage as best he could.

Today's pleasure craft usually place the galley in a far more convenient location, but often ignore the way a galley functions, and fail to include such basics as a galley hatch, always provided on working vessels of yesteryear.

Aft galleys—just off center of the main companionway—seem to be the most popular design, especially aboard sailboats. They can be well ventilated and they are handy for a cook doubling as a deckhand. As they usually face fore or aft, the location makes it easiest for the cook to keep balanced. However, aft galleys sit in line of the heaviest traffic. To avoid feet in the soup pot, add shelves and counter space so the companionway stairs are not needed as work space. If the galley spreads across the companionway and the cook lacks eight-foot arms, think seriously about transferring all of the galley gear to one side or the other. Converting the standard L-shaped galley into a U is another worthwhile alteration which gives the cook additional work space.

Aft galleys may interfere with radio and navigational equipment and vice versa. Before you get underway make certain that both departments are clear of each other, and that even the heaviest iron pot will not offset the compass.

Midship galleys eliminate traffic problems, leave the captain plenty of room for charts and navigational gear, and usually pro-

Keep the cook from rolling with the waves by installing ceiling handles, a simple life-line rig and non-skid strips on the deck.

vide more counter space than aft galleys. However, they tend to be stuffy, may make provisioning difficult, and, as they are nearly always against either the port or starboard bulkheads, are more vulnerable to pitching and rolling.

If there is not at least a small galley hatch—and usually there is not—one should be cut. This provides adequate ventilation and greatly simplifies loading which, in the case of *ice*, can be dangerous if a 50-pound block must be dragged down the companionway and across the main cabin.

Compensate for pitching and rolling by installing extra stormrails (fiddleboards), a gimbaled stove, and a belt lifeline rig that keeps the cook from flying across the cabin or onto the stove top. A nonskid deck in front of the stove and handles or safety straps bolted to the ceiling also help the cook; they are essential if any cooking is to be done underway.

The Sink and The Stove

A sink, a stove and an icebox or refrigerator are the basic components of any galley; accompanied by a modicum of counter space and storage, cooking potential is limited only by the energy and imagination of the cook. Specific placement of equipment is a matter of personal taste; however, regardless of the arrangement, the entire galley should be within arm's reach of the pivoting cook.

The sink's most important feature is its size. If it is not large enough to fill your pots and wash your dishes, replace it with one that is. Installing a larger sink is not always a simple job, but it is well worth the effort in the long run. A tall bar faucet is another excellent means of providing extra sink space.

It is much easier to conserve water if the sink has both fresh-

Cooks who like to bake will find stove-top ovens (many of which fold for storage) a most useful accessory.

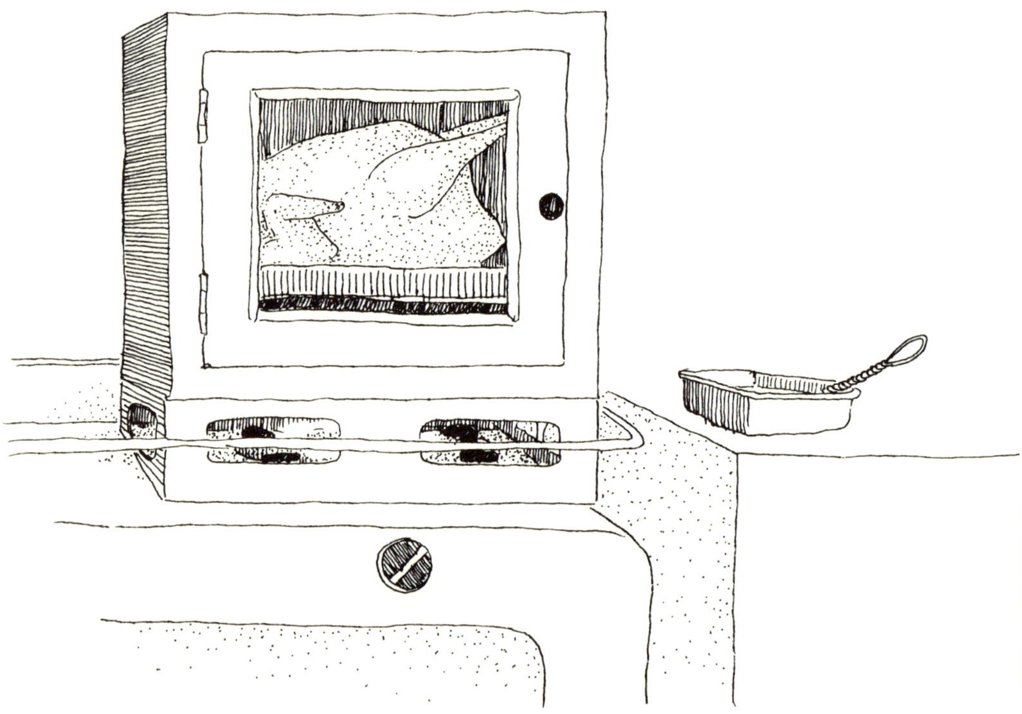

water and saltwater taps; once offshore, saltwater is safe for both cooking and washing.

Manual water pumps are a little more work than pressurized systems, but they simplify maintenance and tend to make the crew more aware that they are tapping a limited water supply. The size of your vessel will of course dictate the number of electricity-dependent accessories you carry. Personally, there are many power items I would select before pressurized water. Also, as a safety factor, it is imperative to have a water supply available that is independent of your electrical system.

A hot water tap falls into the same category as pressurized flow—it is unnecessary. Unless you have a heat-exchange on your engine and plan to use it, plan ahead for your hot water needs. An electric razor is simpler and draws less electricity than a water heater for shaving water. For longer cruises, when both hot water and electricity are at a premium, a beard is the best solution.

The stove is the nerve center of the galley. More than any other single piece of equipment, the stove can make time spent in the galley a good or bad experience. There are myriad models on the market. Some would be right at home in the cockpit of a spaceship, whereas others are best suited to being tossed overboard. Into this latter category I place the portable models that are not designed to be secured when in use. They are fine for camping trips, but aboard a boat they are dangerous because they slide around during cooking. If you must rely on such a portable, secure it with battens. I also recommend battens for models designed to nest in place of storage compartment covers; anything so unlikely to be needed that it can be stored beneath a hot stove is best left ashore.

The most practical stoves are permanently installed and gimbaled. Any gimbaled item—stove, table, etc.—should have pegs so that it may be secured when not in use. It is helpful to be able to cover the stove burners with a fitted top when they are not in use; just remember, this additional counter space is available only for prep work and for cold meals when the stove won't be needed. Even if the stove is augmented by a hibachi, hot plate or Sterno stove, if it is to cook for more than one person, it should have at least two burners. Stoves with more than two burners tend to discourage careful planning, take up extra room, dirty more pots, and burn more fuel.

All stoves aboard any vessel should be fitted with railings so that pots will neither slide nor spill. These can be set up to fit virtually any stove and are necessary even if very little cooking is done underway. The wake of a passing vessel is enough to dump dinner even when you are on the hook.

Fuels

The fuel a stove fires on is even more important than the design of the stove. There are four basic types of shipboard fuels: solid, liquid, gas and electricity. Each has advantages and disadvantages which should be carefully weighed, even though you have one type already in use. The fuel you burn may hamper your success in the galley and increase your work load.

Solid fuels are most popular with old-timers and purists, especially with those who sail northern waters in winter. For most vessels, however, solid fuels are impractical. They take a long time to fire and thus are usually best kept going all day. They require venting through a Charlie Noble, or smokestack, which, if not carefully installed and fitted with a cooling pan, becomes a deck hazard. They must also be able to be sealed during rough weather. With the exception of Sterno and other forms of canned heat, too expensive for general use, solid fuels produce ashes which, at best, are messy to handle. Wood takes up too much storage space for most vessels and the fire requires regular stoking. Coal also demands attention and nearly always leaves the cook red-eyed from fumes. Also, a most important consideration, both coal and wood are often hard to come by in remote ports of call—a sure sign of modern times.

Liquid fuels are my favorite. Some take a little longer to fire than either gas or electricity, but are by no means the bother of either coal or wood. Stoves operating on liquid fuels are logically simple to operate and easy to fix when something goes wrong.

Of the liquid fuels, kerosene and diesel oil are the least expensive, but they are best suited to larger stoves. Because both kerosene and diesel oil can be gravity-fed, they eliminate the stoking required by solid fuels. However, as large stoves are most efficient when fired throughout the day, kerosene and diesel oil are, like solid fuels, most popular in northern waters where the stove doubles as a winter heating unit.

Also, a major drawback to diesel oil is that the most efficient diesel stoves incorporate a small electric blower which, although drawing nowhere near as much electricity as an electric stove, ties cooking into the electrical system.

Alcohol is the most practical liquid fuel for smaller boats. It is by far the most popular fuel among sailors because it quickly provides a hot, fast-cooking flame that requires little attention and is safely extinguishable with water. Of all the liquid-fuel stoves, those that fire on alcohol are probably easiest to maintain.

Perfect for the midnight watch: a small gimbaled stove allows crew and guests to heat coffee, soups and other snacks during the cook's off-hours.

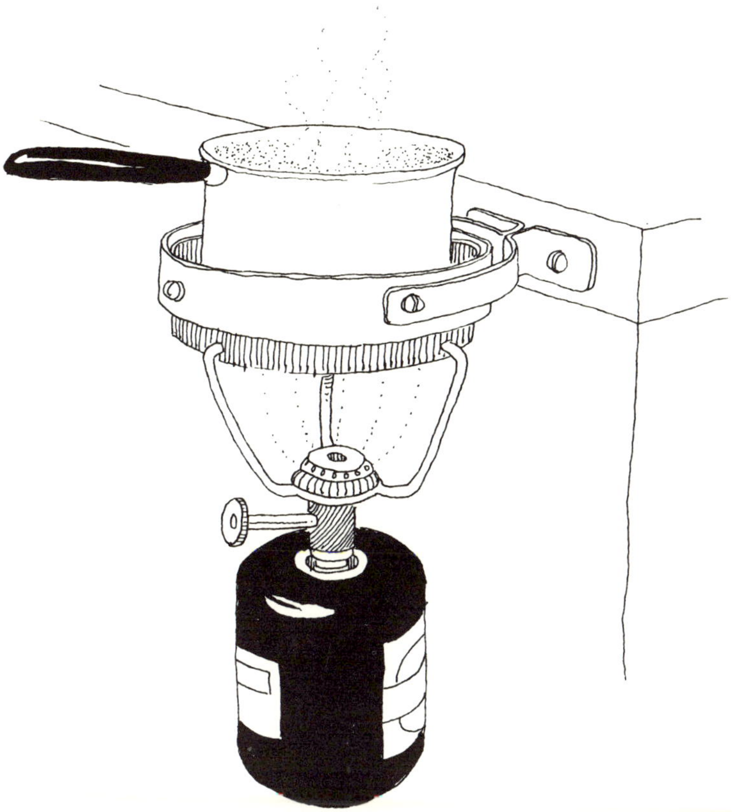

Moderation is the key to safe, efficient operation of an alcohol burner. Overfilling the tank may build up too much pressure, thereby causing the fuel to overflow. However, unlike other liquid fuels, alcohol will quickly and totally evaporate, so that even if fumes require evacuation of the galley, in only a short time the galley will again be clean and safe to use. Overpriming is another practice to avoid. It will cause a flare-up which must then be allowed to burn down, a good reason to make certain that nothing hangs above the stove. If the burner is clean, the tank properly filled and the fuel fresh, an alcohol stove should fire fairly quickly and then run evenly for hours.

Gas is without a doubt the easiest fuel to use aboard, and propane stoves are versatile and virtually trouble-free. Unfortunately, because of the extremely volatile nature of the gas, propane is about as welcome aboard most vessels as a collision with a fire ship. Propane is heavier than air; if at any time the tank fails to vent properly or a leak develops in the line, the gas will sink to the bilge, where even the smallest spark will cause it to explode. Placing the tank on the forward deck may not solve the problem because there is still a great likelihood the gas will find its way below. Several recently designed vessels contain the tanks in a leakproof, properly vented stern compartment, insulated and isolated from the rest of the vessel. The manufacturers contend that this system overcomes any serious objections to shipboard use of gas. The Coast Guard, however, still refuses to allow propane, regardless of the system used, on any commercial passenger-carrying vessel because of the extremely volatile nature of the gas.

Electricity is second only to gas in convenience, but because electric burners have a limited range of temperatures and tend to cool slowly, I find them less desirable than a flame for cooking. Electric stoves are, however, easy to operate, and although they are complicated to repair if something goes wrong, in my experience they rarely break down. The obvious drawback to cooking with electricity is that it requires power supplied by either a generator or a shore-line. Though electric stoves tend to be reliable, a vessel's electrical system is not. It is bad enough to be deprived of power, without also having to do without food.

If you have adequate power most of the time, but don't want to depend solely on electricity for cooking, there are several dual-fuel stoves on the market that cook with either electricity

Install fiddleboards or railings on all shelves and put sturdy latches on all cabinet doors.

or alcohol. This is a system highly desirable for powerboats; it greatly increases their versatility by lessening their dependence on electricity.

Storage

Adequate storage is essential so that provisions can be found when needed. As with counter space, the greater the galley storage area the better. Cupboards with sliding doors and sturdy latches seem to work best, although a few open shelves for spices and other frequently used items are a great help. Both open and cupboard shelves should be fitted with high, scuppered railings so spills are contained yet easily washed out. If open shelves are too small or impractical, due to space limitations, a small netted hammock keeps things handy, visible, and safe from spilling.

Hooks are useful as long as they have safety clips to prevent the spatulas, potholders, or whatever, from slipping off. But make certain that nothing overhangs the stove or requires the cook to reach across a hot burner.

The most common complaint about storage space is not that it is too limited, but that the areas are inaccessible. If your shelves are too dark or too deep, organize provisions in any of the many rectangular rubber or plastic containers on the market, then place them bin by bin into the compartments. An entire container will easily slide forward or lift out, eliminating the chore of pulling everything out, one can at a time, in order to find the peas at the rear. The plastic bins also help confine spills.

Proper organization is the real key to maximizing galley storage area. In a small galley I always keep one storage compartment free, so that I can fill it each morning with the provisions I will need for the day. This saves me from frantic hunts in the middle of preparing a meal, and also allows me to save galley space by storing such items as eggs, vegetables and fruits, which will keep well in any dry compartment, far from the galley.*

Additional Equipment

Hundreds of accessories are available to augment the basic galley. Most are unnecessary space wasters that will rarely be used. A few items, however, are practical and will greatly increase the versatility of the galley.

A small, single-pot stove that uses canned heat for fuel is probably the one most useful addition. Some solo sailors rely on these fast-cooking devices as their only stove.

The most common single-pot stoves use Sterno fuel, come gimbaled, and attach to the galley wall above and out of the way of the counter top. These simple rigs quickly heat everything from soup to babies' bottles and are ideal for preparing coffee,

* For more information on organizing provisions, including important safety tips on storing canned goods, see Chapter Seven on Practical Provisioning.

Toast is best made on an old-time folding toaster.

hot chocolate, or soup between meals—especially during a midnight watch when the cook is asleep.

Many old-fashioned appliances readily adapt to the modern galley, saving time and space. The collapsible oven, now rarely seen outside of Vermont and Maine, will bake bread or, in a pinch, even a roast; it folds for compact storage. The once-common stove-top toaster is another useful appliance. Toast, made from whole-grain bread, settles stomachs and makes up for missed roughage. Like the oven, these toasters fold away when not needed.

The hibachi, or charcoal grill, is another accessory that can greatly increase the variety of your meals. If you plan to carry meat and like the taste of charcoal-broiled food, a hibachi is well worth the effort it requires. Even roasts can be cooked on a hibachi if you have the time and the patience. Set a hood made of several layers of heavy foil over your roast. And use a cooking thermometer because the great variations in cooking conditions make it impossible to predict cooking times accurately.

On the hook, when the wind always blows off the stern, a hibachi will take the cook out of the galley to prepare the meal where all aboard will enjoy watching and smelling the meal as it cooks. Hibachis designed for boat use hang off the stern, over the water, and can be quickly flipped upside down (charcoal is biodegradable) and dumped in case the fire gets out of control or when cooking is finished.

I recommend you do not use starter fluid if it is possible to start the coals without it. However, often if there is any breeze at all, untreated coals won't start. In such cases, it is best to use presaturated coals which are far safer than spraying fluid from a can.

Important! Never use gasoline in place of starter fluid. Gasoline is extremely volatile and even a small amount can cause an explosion with the force of TNT.

Along many areas of the American coastline seagulls are the greatest threat to cooking on a hibachi. Unless you have the patience to stand over the coals waving a broom, it is best to set up a rig that will ward off the gulls. A simple Clorox bottle with fins cut out of the sides will spin on a short pole set out over the hibachi and should do the trick. If the gulls persist, staple strips of aluminum foil to the fins. If two of these fail to discourage the scavengers, or if you frequent seagull havens, sell the hibachi.*

It is impossible to prevent accumulation of grease on a hibachi. The best way to prevent the grease spreading is to store the hibachi in a bucket in the lazeret or similar compartment. This system works well for those who like hibachi cooking. Those who do not contend that no matter what, grease will end up on everything. I use a hibachi often and find it a welcome change of pace for both cook and crew.

Lotus leaf cookery, or the use of an oriental cooking wok, is perhaps the most exciting addition to any galley. A wok is a cone-shaped pot with a wide top and a narrow, nearly flat bottom. Cooking is accomplished by placing a small amount of cooking oil in the wok and heating it to near-smoking. Food is then briefly turned in the oil and then, fully cooked in minutes,

* Incredible as it may sound, I can't help mentioning that many of the sailors I have talked to have told me that the best thing to keep the gulls off are rubber snakes on the deck—the snakes you find in toy stores. They say one or two and the gulls will never come near the boat. Owls, like the decoys available from hunting outfitters, are also said to do the trick. I've never seen either of these two methods in action, but they are worth a try before you give up to the gulls.

is pushed up the sloping sides while the next item or portion is prepared. A wok takes up only a little more room than an ordinary pot, yet it can quadruple the variety of dishes served. Not only does the wok cook amazingly quickly, it retains maximum food value, cleans easily, and is a snap to use.

At first glance, a wok looks unstable, which is possibly why it is not in more common use aboard boats in the Western hemisphere. Actually, it is not unstable at all. The wok's narrow base sits in a ring, called a collar, which holds it slightly above the heat source. By shopping around it is possible to find a wok with a collar that hugs your burner and helps to hold the wok steady. Also, select a wok that has handles—most have—so that you can further secure it by running screendoor springs through the handles and down to the stove's storm railings, just as you would for any pot. The springs take only a minute to rig and the wok won't budge no matter how heavy the seas.*

Although a wok cooks with very hot oil, this kind of cooking is considered better and more wholesome than frying. Meats

Discourage sea gulls by cutting fins in the bottom of a plastic container; attach strips of foil, and set it spinning on a dowel stick near the hibachi.

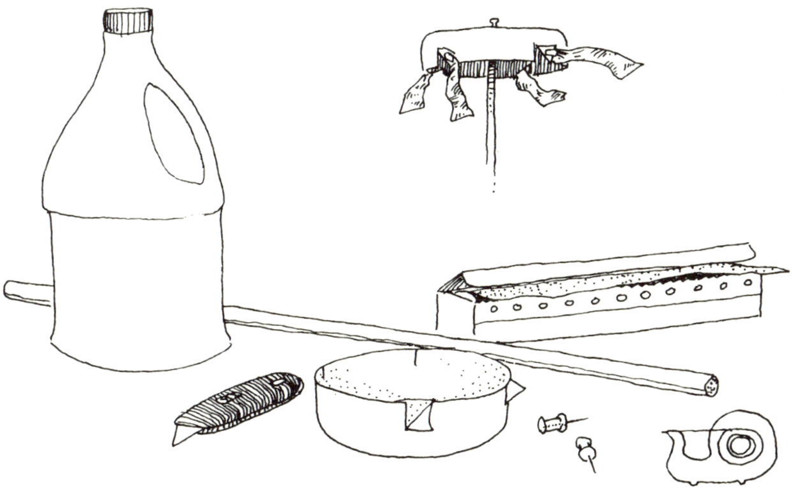

* In the South Pacific, wok users often have the collar permanently spot-welded to the wok, making it even more stable.

An oriental cooking wok will add infinite diversity to meals prepared in the galley. Secured with screendoor springs, a wok won't budge regardless of how rough the swells.

and vegetables are so briefly submerged in such hot oil that virtually no oil is absorbed by the food. In contrast, the amount of oil absorbed by conventional frying can be a major problem, and fried foods are liable to be less than settling on sea-tossed stomachs. The wok enjoys a further advantage because of the small amount of oil used and the high sides of the wok; there is little danger of spattering or spilling.

Although individual preferences may suggest additional galley accessories, I believe that, properly used, the above items, augmented by the pots and pans below, will allow the cook the greatest freedom possible aboard a small to medium-size vessel.

Pots and Pans

Large frypan with deep sides
Small frypan with deep sides
Large pot—at least 4 quarts
Medium-sized pressure cooker
Medium-sized double boiler
Large kettle with whistle—for boiling water quickly

Serving Gear

Serving at sea offers several options. It is possible to duplicate shore table settings if you are willing to pay the price, both in terms of actual cost and in time spent in extra care of breakables. It is also possible to do the disposable route and rough it with paper in order to eliminate all dishwashing. However, as few boaters have either the finances or the time to go the expensive route, and as there is no escaping having to clean pots and pans—and washing dishes is only a little more work, some sort of compromise would seem to be the best solution.

Generally speaking, aboard medium-size boats the aesthetics of serving ware is inversely proportional to its practicality.

China, considered the most attractive dinnerware ashore, makes little sense except on an ocean liner. Metal, such as pewter and aluminum can be very attractive, but it is heavy and expensive, cannot be used to store foods in, and is rarely long-lasting. (Aboard the *Bill of Rights* pewter was used for its authenticity, and it was both attractive and generally serviceable. However, without a messman and a bevy of passengers willing to set and later wash the heavy dishes, and without a captain willing to replace them when they fell apart, which pewter sometimes does after heavy use, I would have demanded paper plates inside of a week on the water.)

Plastic is the most popular dinnerware on pleasure craft. It can be purchased in a variety of strengths and designs at a variety of prices. It seems to stand up fairly well, is practical for both hot and cold items, washes as easily as other materials, and can be replaced relatively inexpensively.*

Paper is the final option. Paper plates are excellent time-savers for many lunches and some dinners. If backed by reusable wicker holders, paper plates work fairly well and are not unattractive. Wicker holders also reduce costs by making it possible to use the least expensive paper products. Paper plates are without a doubt handy and should be carried aboard and used when practical. However, they cannot replace bowls for soups,

* I omit from this discussion the very thin plasticware and rubberware which will not stand up to repeated use and is a waste of money no matter what the conditions.

stews and such, do not lend themselves to cutting, and are too costly to be used all the time.

Metal cup and plates also work fairly well. Unfortunately, metal conducts heat very efficiently and thus metal serving gear often gets too hot to handle.

Utensils

Though plastic is best suited for dinner plates, it is least desirable for flatware. Plastic utensils are short-lived and difficult to clean properly. Stainless steel is relatively inexpensive, considering its durability. Moreover, it can be sterilized by boiling should the need arise. Reasonably priced stainless utensils would seem to be the most practical utensils for shipboard use.

Cleaning Up

The best way to make cleaning up fast and simple is to dirtproof the galley ahead of time. Today, most galleys come from the factory built of fiberglass; although they lack the beauty of wood, they are long-lasting and scrub down easily. If your galley is built of wood or any other surface that is liable to collect grease and resist detergents, cover it with hard Formica or stainless steel—the ideal galley surface. Make certain that any new counter top is properly installed, or moisture will collect between the old and new layers, causing dry rot and mold.

Varnish all wood, such as handrails or decorative trim. Below decks, varnish will stand up for a long time and will wipe clean with just a soapy sponge.

Set up a practical trash system, hang a paper towel dispenser near the sink (keep the dispenser filled), and invest in stainless-steel sponges and other time-saving cleanup devices you use in mainland kitchens. Also, keep a variety of soaps and cleaners on hand for the various tasks that may arise.

NOTE: *A word of caution—select cleaners that produce the fewest fumes. Confined below deck some cleansers, such as ammonia, can produce extremely unpleasant gases and should be used rarely. It is imperative in such close quarters that all aboard are careful not to mix chemicals; for example, the combination of ammonia and chlorine is lethal.*

Take care that all cutting and chopping is done on a block that won't scratch or splinter and that will protect the counter tops; once nicked and chipped, counter tops will be much more difficult to clean. Composition chopping blocks, required by most health departments for restaurant use, work best.

Condense all garbage as best you can. Remove the tops and bottoms of "iron rations" and flatten them. Crush paper and plastic containers.

Boiling water, seawater or freshwater, is one of the best cleaners, and its price is certainly right. If you need more space for water than the sink provides, use a wooden bucket placed on the counter. A wet rag under the bucket will help prevent it sliding.

If your galley is properly dirtproofed you should have no difficulty cleaning as you cook, with a final once-over when the meal is finished. I always wash what few pots and pans I use before I join the others for dinner, and I always take a turn at the helm while someone else goes below to do the dishes.

Chapter Three

KEEPING YOUR COOL

One week aboard the *Bill of Rights* during November, when it was already too cold to stir from my bunk until the sun was well up, we took aboard a lady journalist from some place outside of New England. I am still not certain what sort of a story she was writing; all I remember is granting her request for extra yogurt and her banging on the fo'c'sle hatch cover as she woke me to get it for her nearly every night between 2 and 3 A.M.—all because I was responsible for anything that came out of the icebox. This is a cook's responsibility which I agree with under normal circumstances, but during that week I learned at least one reason why some sailors prefer to travel without cold storage.

Cold milk; ice for cocktails; "we must put in for more ice;" maybe doing without an icebox or a refrigerator really is a good idea . . .

Well, doing without cold storage is definitely a realistic option aboard a boat. In fact, it is fairly common among sailors and power boaters who travel long distances without access to ice or shore-lines. Despite generators and modern electric refrigeration, the limitations of ocean travel make it sensible for many boaters to readjust their perspectives back about 100 years the minute they step off soundings in anything less than a trans-Atlantic power yacht.

Sailboats are usually without ice after about six days, and power boats must curb their use of electricity also. But even without cold storage, if you make a few simple adjustments and are willing to go without ice in cocktails, you can eat just as well as you did with a refrigerator ashore.

A great many foods will keep for at least two weeks—without cold storage. They are diverse, nutritious, easy to prepare, and require no maintenance. If you go this route, unless you brag, no one need know you are functioning without an icebox.*

For most boaters, however, the icebox or refrigerator is the third primary piece of galley equipment. If you are rarely more than three days from a civilized port even if you stop only just long enough to pick up some ice, there is no reason to do without the advantages of cold storage. On all but the smallest factory-built boats, an icebox, at least, is standard equipment.

The Icebox

Side-opening boxes are, to me, the most practical because they are the easiest to load, inventory, and use. Unfortunately, a side-opening box is not as efficient as a top-opener due to the great loss of cold air when it is opened. Another major drawback is that if a door gets loose and a shelf slides forward, everything tumbles all over the place. Thus strong latches and railed shelves are imperative for side-opening iceboxes.

Though I prefer side-openers, most boats come with top-opening chests. Shelves are usually solid, molded fiberglass that cannot be removed, and many boxes are too deep for easy access.

As long as an ice chest has a drain, shortcomings can be overcome, regardless of the design. If shelves are solid, drill a dozen ¼- to ½-inch holes into each to allow for draining and ventilation. With top openers attach a nylon strap with a ring on the far end to the chest cover, so that the cover can be hooked open, leaving both hands free to delve below.

If the icebox is to be useful for longer than one-day trips, it must have a drain so it can be emptied of accumulated meltings. A reservoir of water spoils food by soaking it and also tends to retain heat and warm the chest. Some chests have an open cock system that allows continuous drainage into the bilge

* The two major disadvantages of not having cold storage are lack of ice for drinks and, after four days, a lack of fresh meat. The latter can be compensated for, in part, with fish. Also, the texture and flavor of meat can be supplied with properly prepared canned, dried and dehydrated meats as well as with other high-protein foods.

Holes in ice-box trays and bins will help drain meltings and improve air circulation.

or overboard; others have a valve that allows drainage either into the bilge or a sump tank. To many boaters, draining into the bilge is unacceptable because it can make for a foul hold. I have never experienced this problem, but I imagine it depends upon the individual vessel and the amount of spilling that combines with the water in the chest. Regardless, the chest should be drained at least twice a day to keep cooling at peak efficiency.

Items too deep in the icebox to reach easily should be arranged in the same type of bins used for hard-to-get-at shelf storage areas. Make use of the many sizes and colors available to develop a system that best utilizes your space and helps you to identify the bin you are looking for. Make certain, however, that any bins in the path of dripping ice water have holes like the shelves, so they won't fill and soak the entire contents, making them too heavy to lift out without a crane.

Ice

The storage of ice is logical and requires no great amount of planning. Heat rises, cold sinks, so ice is best stored as high in the chest as possible. If at all possible, prevent the water dripping onto the food even if it is necessary to mold temporary gutters out of aluminum foil; water will spoil food even faster than heat, and every box should have a grate to keep food above the meltings.

Bulk ice melts more slowly than cubes because there is less surface area exposed. For this reason purchase ice for drinks separately in cubes. If cubes are drawn often, it is a good idea to augment the ice chest with a well-insulated ice bucket which helps to limit the number of times the main chest must be opened.* Under all circumstances *avoid chipping ice inside the chest!* The chances of the pick puncturing a side and ruining the box are too great.

If you carry your drinking water from a spring near your home port, it makes sense to freeze it ahead of time in plastic bottles so it can double as a coolant, and you can drink the meltings every day.

Always use a heavy canvas or burlap bag or tongs to handle ice. I've seen a twenty-pound block, dropped by accident, split a two-inch steel rod.

Storing Food in the Ice Chest

All foods except canned goods should be rewrapped before being stored in the icebox. Transfer milk and other cartoned beverages into plastic containers; like plastic bins, they come in myriad sizes, shapes and colors to suit your individual needs. Most boaters find that containers that have tight screw caps and are squared for compact storage work best.

Meat, fish and vegetables kept in cold storage should be removed from their store packaging and wrapped in aluminum foil. Cover the foil with a plastic wrap or bag to keep out the moisture.

* This also preserves the galley as the bailiwick of the cook and the cook alone—a firm rule of mine.

Canned goods seem to stand up very well, although jars are more convenient as they are resealable. Check all vacuum-packed items for bulges indicating contamination, especially if they have been stored for any length of time. As with cans stored in the bilge or any other place where there is a likelihood that they will get wet, remove all labels and mark the contents with a waterproof crayon.

As long as you remember that iceboxes are wet storage, the system is logical. Use plenty of aluminum foil, plastic wraps and plastic containers, and carry extra wrapping materials so you can take the same care when storing leftovers. If at all possible, precool all icebox items before storing them in the chest.

Electric Refrigerators

The great advantage to having an electric refrigerator on board is that it eliminates the problem of ice and its concomitant wetness. Nonetheless, to assure that foods last their longest, take the same care, as with the icebox, in rewrapping foods ahead of time, though you may safely leave off the extra layer of plastic.

On most boats refrigerator space is at a premium so organize foods accordingly. Precutting meats and vegetables helps save time and space. Depending upon how much time you spend in advance organization of your meals, you may decide to store foods either by types, i.e., meats, vegetables, liquids; or by meals, so that you can quickly grab what you need and shut the door. As with iceboxes, if you use much ice for drinks, transfer it in bulk to an insulated cooler as another step in limiting the number of times the refrigerator door must be opened and closed.

If you have a choice of refrigerators, do not get a self-defrosting model. If it is a model that happens to work well, a self-defrosting refrigerator may save you a little work, but it is not worth the extra electricity it draws.

If is important to defrost a refrigerator whenever necessary, which is usually more often at sea than ashore due to the extra moisture in the air.

Chapter Four

JURY-RIGGING—TIPS AND TRICKS FOR MAKING DO

Every time I have sailed for more than a week, no matter what the size or shape of the vessel, a pump gives out. Sometimes it's the bilge pump, other times it's been a fuel or water pump, and the most memorable time it was the pump on a marine head. Although I have personally witnessed the demise of over a dozen pumps, not one has had the decency to show even a hint of weakness while still within range of a supply shop. Fortunately, every pump breakdown was successfully jury-rigged until correct replacement parts were available.

Usually, aboard a properly equipped boat, such problems can be mended with items from either the cook's or the captain's ditty bag, combined with some trial and error experimentation and a good deal of patience. There are times, however, when extra resourcefulness is called for and only one's imagination can devise a solution. Once in a desperate attempt to repair a manual water pump, the only access to the vessel's water supply, I discovered that a wine bottle cork (luckily we did have a corkscrew), trimmed with a knife, can be used to replace a worn rubber gasket if the problem is a broken seal. I now recommend corks of various sizes and shapes as a staple for any cook's ditty bag.

All it takes is a little ingenuity and a box of select odds and ends, and just about anything can be jury-rigged. Remember, though, that jury-rigging is a temporary solution, only to be used when it is impossible to make permanent repairs on the spot. Never jury-rig when proper replacement parts are available and always replace a jury-rig with a correct rig as soon as possible.

Not only does extensive jury-rigging make for a sloppy ship, but if left longer than necessary, a jury-rig is likely to complicate needlessly your next *ad hoc* repair.

It is perfectly permissible to identify a faulty design on a piece of equipment and to change it so it functions compatibly with your needs; however, this requires a complete understanding of the manufacturer's design and intentions and comes under the category of "redesigning." Redesigning should not be confused with jury-rigging, which is strictly an emergency repair.

Just as the galley and all its gear are the cook's responsibility, so is galley jury-rigging. A good cook realizes that whether it's a failing water pump or a broken latch, breakdowns are bound to occur away from port, and they must be repaired as soon as possible if it is to be meals as usual. Even in a galley equipped with the simplest gear, carefully inspected before setting out, there may be unavoidable breakdowns. The trick is to accept and expect the unexpected. Like so many other situations at sea, with a little care and forethought the effects of a breakdown can usually be limited.

Don't depend on the captain's tool chest; every galley should keep a ditty bag containing materials and tools for basic repairs.

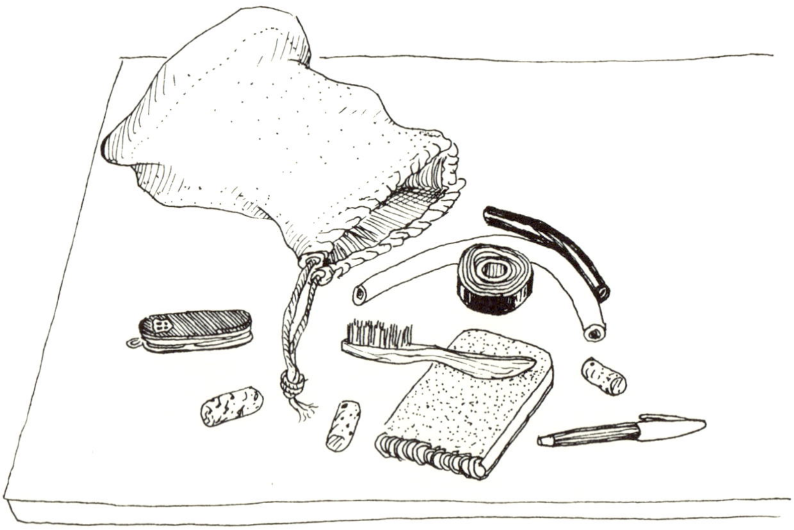

The first step for any cook is to become familiar with the galley and its equipment. Manufacturer's instruction booklets should be read and then kept handy. Next, make certain that the galley has its own ditty bag, tailored to galley needs. The cook must not depend upon forays into the engine toolbox, but should be self-sufficient, so that both the captain's and the cook's fix-it supplies are there when needed; it is impossible to maintain an accurate inventory unless access is limited.

A galley's repair-gear inventory begins with a good Swiss army knife, complete with a can opener. A corkscrew is also handy and can save hours trying to open a bottle with an awl. Waterproof tape, at least 1 inch wide, is a second must. Also include corks, springs and hooks, a thread-sealer, Liquid Steel or some other epoxylike glue, wire, clamps, sandpaper and a toothbrush-size wire brush. A small toolbox with several different screwdrivers for regular screws and Phillips Screws, a small hammer, vice grips, an adjustable wrench and pliers is another excellent idea. The toolbox should also contain a variety of screws, metal and rubber washers, a tape measure, a pen and some paper.

Extra rubber hoses can be used to repair water and fuel lines with leaks too large to seal with tape. Rubber bands and some thin but strong string are old standbys, as are a needle and thread, pins and several small blocks of wood that can be cut into wedges. Stow a small can of simple household lubricating oil in a leakproof container, along with a tube of caulking which should be periodically checked to make sure it is fresh, and a can of liquid graphite.

In additon to the above standbys, it is well to stock any parts that you can anticipate wearing out. These will depend upon the specific equipment in your galley, but may include items such as filters for fuel lines, grease trays that fit beneath burners, extra potholders, or anything else, large or small, simple or complex.

Simplicity is another key to jury-rigging. Never attempt a complicated rig when a simple one will do. If you run out of soap, before you start robbing the head of the last bar available for washing hands, wipe down plates, pots and utensils as best you can, then sterilize them by boiling them in seawater; it may take a little longer, but from a health standpoint there is no better way to clean. After the water reaches a boil, continue to boil for 15 to 20 minutes to assure sterility.

There are usually at least two ways to do everything and if you keep this in mind you can often sidestep a problem without any jury-rigging at all. When you plan meals and organize your galley gear, keep an open mind: be flexible. Most importantly, don't panic! Even jury-rigging takes care and patience, and if the hurry is too great you will create more problems than you will solve.

Chapter Five

COOKING UP A STORM

Everything was all set. In spite of stormy weather and five-foot swells, I had made and set out lunch without a hitch. Hot soup, a light salad, and fixings for hot turkey sandwiches were all lined up presentable as could be on the long, gimbaled table in the main salon. Down the companionway came the passengers, navigating the heeling cabin sole as though it were a funhouse floor. Then a larger-than-average swell rocked the boat and a passenger instictively reached for the gimbaled table instead of the bench bolted to the deck. The table tilted fifty degrees, dumping the passenger and the entire lunch setup, including the salad oil, which proceeded to coat the cabin floor, sending everyone, including myself, slipping and sliding from bulkhead to bulkhead hopelessly trying to regain our balance. Not only was everything a grand mess, but lunch was spread across the cabin and all aboard were hungrier than before.

To make a long afternoon short, I somehow managed, and no one went without lunch.

The rougher the weather, the more smoothly a galley must function. As winds swing 'round to the northeast and seas begin to roll, not only is the unexpected to be expected, but chilling weather, the tension of a storm, and the increased work load for all hands makes the warmth and energy supplied by food all the more important.

At times like these, when everyone is hungry but no one feels like eating, a meal needs to be both tastily appealing and as settling as possible. The food should be simple and straightforward for the cook to prepare and keep hot—all day, if necessary—so it can be eaten whenever anyone gets the time and the urge.

A few simple modifications in the galley and the addition of several pieces of extra gear will keep your storm cooking on an

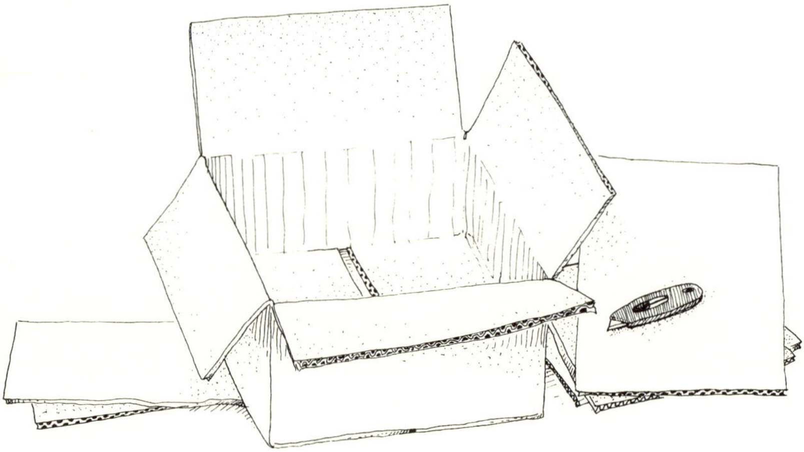

Corrugated cardboard is the best temporary solution to large oily or greasy spills. Placing cardboard on the spill prevents slipping until time permits thorough cleaning.

even keel. The number of changes you make will, to a large extent, depend on the original placement and setup of your galley. Shortcomings become proportionately difficult to cope with as the seas rise.

First, secure all stores and gear. Plastic bins, hooks with safety clips, and sturdy latches that cannot open by themselves are all good ideas. Two strips of molding screwed into the deck about two feet apart and perpendicular to the stove will help the cook to brace. A simple lifeline will also help keep the cook in place, while still allowing free movement and quick exit.

Storms are when stove railings are most important. To augment the railings, loop standard screendoor springs through pot handles and down to the rails. Use only larger pots and pans with high sides; sides twice as high as the depth of the content are ideal.

Keep heavy-duty potholders handy. Though I usually prefer the open square holders, during storms I always wear a glove potholder on one hand so that I am ready to grab a falling hot pot without wasting time reaching for a holder or getting burned. A pair of tongs is also excellent for hot items.

Find a flashlight that is suited to your galley and attach it to a clip so it can hang from your side. Also, make certain the batteries are fresh; salt air seems to weaken them quickly.

Corrugated cardboard should always be available as a temporary solution to oily spills. It will soak up much of the oil and at the same time provide a less slippery surface to move about on. Covering the deck with cardboard was the first step in solving the above case of the breached lunch.

Install a proper fire extinguisher (see Chapter Eight, Safety at Sea) within arm's reach of the stove and between the galley and the nearest exit. Finally, the cook should pack a thick apron and heavy pair of shoes just as a deckhand packs heavy foul-weather rain gear.

After each storm make a checklist of problems encountered so they can be averted before the next storm. Rough weather often creates conditions that must be experienced before proper solutions can be found.

Food for Foul Weather

During storms the byword of the galley is maximum nourishment for minimum volume, as even the heartiest appetites usually decrease. Hot meals are more easily received than cold; even in the summertime, damp weather will chill to the bone.

If the cook's stomach is sturdy and doesn't object to pitching about below, each meal may be individually prepared. However, as it is unlikely that all aboard will eat at the same time, it is usually better to select an item that can be prepared once and then kept ready all day. Soups are fine for warming, for supplemental snacks, and to sustain those too queasy to eat anything more substantial. But unless the soup falls into the category of a stew, it is simply not hearty enough to take the place of a meal.

Something along the order of a basic New England stew with a thick base, served with whole-wheat bread and hot tea, is an ideal heavy-weather meal. It can be kept hot or quickly reheated. It is easy to add extra carrots, potatoes and tomatoes if the supply begins to run low. However, there is no need to stick to a meat stew. Tomatoes, beans and other vegetables can be mixed to provide a meatless dish with just as much nourishment as meat, often in a more digestible form. Another advantage to vegetables is that they can be served before they are thoroughly cooked, increasing roughage and nutrients and making the meal even quicker to prepare.

Chapter Six

ANY PORT IN A STORM

Though there are those who make exceptions, and I have met a few who have survived, it is a rule of the sea that alcohol and saltwater do not mix, and it would be impossible to begin this discussion without saying so. Traditionally, taverns were home to a sailor ashore, but aboard, willingly or not, he was limited to a daily ration of rum, and not without reason.

Aside from the obvious fact that a few shots can dangerously slow thought and reaction time, the sun and the sea can bring other, less obvious, but just as unpleasant effects. Alcohol and exposure to sun are both naturally dehydrating; the combination of the two can completely upset a person's system and make sunstroke more likely. Also, a shot that calmed nerves and intestines ashore, when tossed in a stomach by even the gentlest swells, can kick up a storm with the full fury of a nor'easter in November. Even a headache, one of the most common side effects of alcohol, is multiplied in unpleasantness by every rock of the boat.

Thus the main purpose of alcohol on a boat—hopefully at dockside or on the hook when the day's traveling is over—is to provide a pleasant beverage, slightly mellowing perhaps. It may also enhance appetites, although fresh sea air usually is a step ahead in that department.

Wine

A "good" red wine, stowed beneath the waterline in a hold, cannot be topped at sea. Served without ice at room temperature, a Burgundy, Claret or Chianti will provide everyone with a satisfying beverage before and/or during meals. Though personal preference will naturally prevail, drier wines usually sit better than sweet wines and are more likely to complement any dish. Chianti seems to be most popular when meals are heavy or spicy. Sweet wines are often too sweet and run the risk of dominating a meal. Also one loses interest in them far more quickly than in drier wines.

There is no need for wine to be expensive for it to be a pleasant shipboard beverage, nor is there harm in buying it by the half or full gallon to facilitate storage.

Red wines should be opened at least half an hour before serving to give vent to the mustiness they acquire from standing in the bottle; decanting the wine further serves this purpose.

With a little experimenting it is quite possible to find a staple wine that will take the place of hard liquor. At sea it is perfectly acceptable to have a wine-only bar, even for guests and entertaining. Stocking only wines eliminates the problem of ice, is less expensive, minimizes the quantity of alcohol consumed, and provides an enjoyable change of pace from cocktails that are traditional ashore.

Liquor

If your taste runs to hard liquor even at sea, save yourself a lot of fuss and hassles and don't get too fancy. A limited bar, stocked with gin, Scotch and one other straightforward choice (possibly a bourbon or blend), with dry and sweet vermouth as mixer and apéritif, is more than adequate. Just make certain you carry what you and your steady crew enjoy, plus one or two additional basics, and your bar will be set for any situation, especially if you augment your hard liquor supply with a sturdy dry red wine.

Club soda, tonic water and ginger ale or maybe a sweeter soda are the most you should need in the way of mixers. Otherwise you will find your liquor cabinet taking up more room than all the rest of your supplies put together.

Irish coffee with whiskey is an ideal drink aboard a boat. Either regular or decaffeinated coffee will do. Like all drinks aboard, this mixture should not be made too strong; an ounce of whiskey to four ounces of coffee is a good balance. If you use decaffeinated coffee and serve it at sunset to take the edge off a cool evening—first make sure all the dishes are washed—there is a very good chance that all aboard will be asleep soon thereafter.

Beer

Beer is usually an unsuccessful beverage for all but day sails, as most Americans feel beer isn't any good unless it is really cold, and it does not lend itself to dilution with ice.

If you must carry beer, store it in a separate ice chest and purchase only resealable quart bottles. Not only are these bottles more practical than cans, they also tend to be consumed less quickly because people drink what they feel like instead of automatically consuming the entire can.

Remember, if the liquor setup aboard your boat gets too complicated and begins to take up too much of your time and thought—turn it over to the captain. Your primary concern is food!

Liquor for Cooking

Vermouth and a dry red wine are basic components of a galley liquor closet; they should be separate from the bar to save confusion and to assure that the Burgundy does not wind up missing in the middle of preparing beef Stroganoff.

Vermouth has long been used by long-distance ocean cooks to add interest to dull items. Even already interesting dishes often benefit from vermouth's unexpected (and rarely discernible) flavor. Add it to a dish everyone has had before when they think they know what to expect.

When cooking, alcohol burns off so there is no reason why it cannot be used in preparing dishes for lunches as well as dinners; these dishes will not have a negative effect on the deck crew.

Another favorite wine for cooking is sherry, not a cream or dry sherry, but a medium sherry that will blend into rather than overcome a dish. Sherry can be added to virtually any dish with almost guaranteed success, but it is best blended with butter. The trick is not to use it too often; it should always be a surprise. When people ask you for your recipe, generously give it to them and leave out the sherry so they will never duplicate exactly what you have served them.

Chapter Seven

PRACTICAL PROVISIONING

" 'Were ya, first thing I'd do, mate, is get me 'nuff salt horse an' ruin my hunger," called an old-timer over his shoulder as I was reaching for a tasty, but impractical, tin in a Nova Scotia market. "Forgot ta do that once and near starved on starch an' suga' 'til I come the next port." And the fellow with the sound advice that saved me a few sad days at sea, if not my life, disappeared 'round the corner.

Ashore, shopping for food when you are hungry is a sure way to spend more than you mean to, especially in modern markets where shoppers are lured up and down aisles of attractively packaged goods, many of which are low in food value and high-priced to boot! Before going to sea, shopping on an empty stomach can wind you up in a situation that is downright dangerous. Regardless of how long or short a voyage you plan, follow basic rules of provisioning, and eat heartily before you shop.

Begin by planning exactly what meals you plan to serve from the galley. (Actually writing it down isn't a bad idea.) Then make a list of the provisions those meals require, add beverages, meals for unexpected guests, snacks, food for heavy weather and emergency rations, and you will have a shopping list which will become an inventory when you have checked it against what you already have aboard. Ashore it is usual practice to get the basic idea of a meal in mind and then, list in hand, go out and market. Boating cooks, however, discover—usually the hard way—that meals that fall together nicely in the kitchen, will fall completely apart in the galley.

The provisioning (shopping) list is the key to fitting out. Space is limited, so look over the list, trim where possible, substitute where necessary. Select foods that are versatile and can be used for several meals without becoming boring. After a time or two, shortening the list will come easily.

Follow the cardinal rule of provisioning: *every edible item must have a purpose.* There is no room aboard a boat for empty calories or fillers. Too many boaters, despite long years on the water, still shop for the galley with the same haphazard methods they get away with in the kitchen. As a result, too many boaters return from a "vacation" at sea in much worse condition than when they left, because the "healthy" activity, combined with a less-than-healthy diet, depleted their reserves. Always keep nutrition in mind when you are provisioning a boat.

Without diving into the realm of "health" foods, you can take simple steps to assure a healthy diet. (I do not mean to suggest there is anything wrong with the diets of "health" food folks; in fact many of these diets include the same staples carried by solo trans-Atlantic sailors.) Just keep the daily, if not the meal-by-meal, menu "balanced"—the old rule of thumb: protein, green vegetable, carbohydrate, and variety.

Vegetables and fruits, fresh preferably, then dried, lastly canned, are your best bet. They are high in food value, versatile, combine well with other foods, or stand alone. Chosen carefully and served in moderation, they will not churn wave-tossed stomachs.

Protein is not, as we Americans tend to forget, synonymous with meat. So even if there is no refrigeration and no opportunity to resupply for a long while, it is not imperative to stow and serve canned meats. Personally, I like many canned meats; I have often served glazed canned ham with a pineapple sauce without anyone, I think, knowing it was from a can. It is my opinion that, used sparingly, they help diversify a shipboard menu.* However, meats are expensive and as there are many other sources of whole protein, I see no reason why meat must be *the* source. Nor do I think meat need be served at every dinner.

Milk, cheese, soybeans and grains are also excellent suppliers of protein and have far better keeping qualities than meats.

* Though fresh meats and vegetables are used in most of the recipes, canned equivalents may be substituted. This will, of course, shorten cooking times and depending on your palate, may or may not detract from the flavor.

Fish, although it keeps as poorly as meat, is another excellent source of protein and is often readily available on a boat.

Sweets may be necessary to keep the crew happy, but try to avoid processed sugar, candy and sweet cookies. Offer instead fruits, honey, nuts, or even raw vegetables if they just seem to be looking for something to munch on between meals. Replace chocolate, carried as a source of instant energy by too many boaters, with bananas. Yes, bananas! Although both chocolate and bananas quickly raise the blood-sugar level, the effects of chocolate wear off, leaving a person less energetic than when he started. Bananas do not drain your reserves and will never give you a letdown feeling.

Beverages are needed as liquid for the body to function properly, but they can also be a source of nourishment. They should be planned and served with these points in the cook's mind, even if everyone else thinks they are just "quenching their thirst." Remember that alcohol—volume as well as proof counts—tends to be dehydrating, offsetting its value as a carbohydrate. Tea has a fair amount of caffeine and coffee has twice as much, which may or may not have an adverse effect on some people. Hot chocolate is excellent for warming. It is lower in caffeine than coffee but has little food value. Milk is the most nutritious drink. Juices can be a good source of vitamin C and other vitamins as well. Drinking water is perhaps the best beverage there is, and also the simplest to carry. If the crew shies away from water because the tanks, clean as they may be, impart an unpleasant flavor, there are taste filters available that will solve the problem. One filter usually lasts a year.

Details of Planning

Remember that it's no crime to keep notes and lists. Plan each sail's menus individually by asking the following questions and carefully considering the answers as you select your provisions.*

* Don't fall into another common trap by relying on a "standard" group of meals that "work for you when cooking on a boat." This is just another way of saying you are in a rut and asking everyone to put up with repetition.

Galley of the *Bill of Rights*: ice chest, Shipmate stove and water pump. Even without electricity, an ideal set up to prepare meals for thirty or more!

What equipment is aboard? Is there an oven, a refrigerator, how many stove burners? Is there a pressure cooker, a wok? What storage areas are available to the cook?

Where are you going and for how long? Will the weather be hot or cold, rough or calm? Will there be opportunities to resupply along the way? Will there be fishing or a chance to gather shellfish? Even if the answer to this last one is a confident "yes," don't count on it!

Who will be aboard—children (extra milk)? If at all possible contact everyone and find out if anyone has any allergies or special diets that will prevent eating certain foods. (I try to limit the answer to allergies because if I include "strong dislikes" too often the list is unmanageably long.) Allergies are a different matter from dislikes, however, and although I feel it is the responsibility of persons who have allergies, or who are on low-salt, low-sugar, or other special diets, to let me know, I find that forgetfulness or embarrassment often prevents their doing so. The best way to prevent problems arising after casting off is to ask the questions myself.

Is company anticipated?

What sort of sailing are you in for? Though all activity on the water creates healthy appetites, racing, long hauls, night watches and captains who insist on refinishing the brightwork between tacks, all will have a definite affect on the amount of food consumed.

Ask the captain if emergency supplies are aboard. Most vessels, even those that only cruise coastal waters, have a supply of rations, but it never hurts to make sure. This is one area where I always act on my own even if the captain's answer is "No, we won't need them."

Also ask the captain if it is he or you who will stock the liquor locker.

Once these questions are answered and a provisions list has been culled from the menus, then and only then are you ready to shop. If you will be on the water for more than a weekend (or will be setting out every weekend) look into food cooperatives where you can buy larger quantities of most everything for far less than at regular markets. Some ports have boating supply stores that sell foods specifically for use at sea. These are tax-free and thus less expensive. Even in regular supermarkets you can sometimes get a good break by buying the largest sizes of canned and boxed goods. However, don't buy the largest sizes just for the sake of saving money. It is best to avoid waste by purchasing sizes that are in line with the portions you will be cooking. The fewer leftovers on a boat, the better.

Wherever you buy, make certain that the foods are fresh. Check the dates stamped on perishables; the freshest containers are usually shelved in back or at the bottom of the pile. Don't be afraid to reach for these. Dates are especially important on dairy products like milk, eggs and cheese.

Get bananas, melons, tomatoes, and other fresh fruits and vegetables a little on the unripe side; they will ripen with time, can be stored without refrigeration, and will be ready to use when you need them.

Examine all canned goods. Don't buy any cans that look swollen, a sign of contamination. Avoid cans with dents as this may be an indication that the vacuum seal has been broken.

In general, hard foods, Cheddar cheeses, turnips and other firm vegetables and fruits such as apples and pears, tend to keep better than softer types.

Think ahead about how an item will be stowed before you buy it. With the variation today in the way foods are prepared and packaged, some brands and products are probably better suited to your needs than others.

Jars have an advantage over cans because they are resealable, but they are also heavier and breakable. Even if you are careful to buy only containers made of especially sturdy glass. They can be a hazard. The plastic containers most often used for dairy products appear to be ideal because they are strong and resealable and take up little room in the trash. Unfortunately, foods that come packaged in these containers often taste like the containers; taste them at home before taking them on a voyage.*

How to Stow What

The keeping quality of an item can be greatly enhanced, or it can be destroyed, by the way it is stowed. Eggs, for example, will keep very well in a dark, cool place without refrigeration, but only if they are dipped into wax to keep the shell from absorbing the moisture which is everywhere on a boat, and if they are turned from day to day to change the position of the yolk. Remember—brown or white, fertilized or unfertilized, all eggs have the same food value. So don't pay more for nothing.

Canned goods will more or less take care of themselves so long as they are not wet long enough to rust. *However, as a general rule, all canned goods should be stripped of their labels and*

* For the same reason it is a good idea to season new plastic bottles and bins before storing food in them. Buy a good quality to begin with, and boil it a few times before using; this usually does the trick.

Avoid the confusion of "mystery" cans and clogged drains when the moisture of bilge storage peels away labels. Before storing, remove the labels, mark the contents with a waterproof crayon and seal with wax.

marked with a waterproof marker as to contents. This will prevent clogging of the bilge drain by loosened labels, a not-unheard-of happening which has caused more than a few vessels to sink. Also, cans left without labels make it nearly impossible to tell what is what. If cans are stored in a place that is likely to be wet for a long period of time, place them in a waterproof plastic bag or dip them into wax after removing the labels and marking them; this extra step will prevent rust and the cans will keep almost indefinitely.

Keep fresh fruits and vegetables in a cool dry place. Replace store wrappings with fresh plastic bags, the kind with holes for air circulation. Examine all fruits and vegetables daily and remove any that are too ripe or have begun to mold.

Hard cheeses will keep very well without refrigeration. Just wrap them tightly to exclude air, and keep in a cool place, out of the sun or other direct heat. Mold will not spoil hard cheese; just trim away the moldy part and the rest is perfectly safe and tasty.

Hard salami will keep best if hung with the opened end down. This allows the fat to seal the opened area, retaining the moisture and freshness of the rest of the roll.

Dried foods should be kept dry. Plastic wrapping is better than a cardboard box.

Fresh meats and all other foods that must be stored in an icebox or a refrigerator should be removed from store packaging, rewrapped and waterproofed. Plastic wraps, aluminum foil and plastic containers are excellent. Just make certain that foods do not get wet or they will spoil even faster than if they had been left out. (See Chapter Three, Keeping Your Cool.)

Transfer fresh milk and other foods that come in waxed cartons into containers that can be turned upside down without spilling. Containers should not be susceptible to being crushed or springing a leak. Plastic, if of good quality, is safer than glass.

Flour, sugar, crackers and all of the many other foods that come cartoned or bagged are far better off in plastic bins which keep out moisture and are more easily accessible.

Spices are safer in metal containers than in glass, but if kept in their store-brought tins, these should be placed in plastic bins because the tins are susceptible to moisture. There are available some plastic containers that screw-fit together into a waterproof stack. If you are willing to go through the bother of transferring spices (the metal containers work fine for me), these stack containers are best as they take up the least room and are handy to use.

Pour oils and sauces into sturdy plastic bottles and jars. (As I said back in Keeping Your Cool, plastic containers are readily available in myriad sizes, shapes and colors.)

If you keep in mind the basic problems of storing and cooking food on a boat, you should, after a few trials and errors, be able to adapt these suggestions to any food that cannot be placed in one of the above categories.

Where to Stow What

Even if you feel that where you stow provisions is logical and straightforward (it is), and comes naturally (it doesn't), take a few moments to sit down and figure out the logistics of storage ahead of time. Otherwise you may find yourself doubling the time it should take to prepare a meal.

Keep things you use often within easy reach of the galley.

There should be shelves and cabinets to make this possible. Heavy goods are less likely to fall if they are kept below waist level; if they are of sufficient quantity, they should be stowed where they will not offset the vessel's center of gravity. All flammables are a hazard unless they are stored outside of the galley; this includes liquor. Paper products run the risk of getting wet unless they are kept above deck level and, ideally, away from a hatch or companionway.

Most importantly, know where you have stowed what. If you make notes on the provisions/inventory list as to where you have put your supplies, there will be no problem finding something in the middle of a meal. There are nearly as many systems of storage as there are galleys. Some cooks use container categories, such as canned goods, bottled goods; others use food categories, such as vegetables, meats, and so on. Regardless of the system you select, be consistent and, no matter how "good" your system is, keep a list.

Consistent organization is the essence of practical provisioning, and lists are the key to organization. Good lists together with good menus make it simple to record successes and failures. Make notes right on your lists and recopy them when they get too crowded. Keep the lists accessible, just in case someone else has to step into the galley and run it.

Seasonings stay put in a small hammock, handily hung within the cook's easy reach.

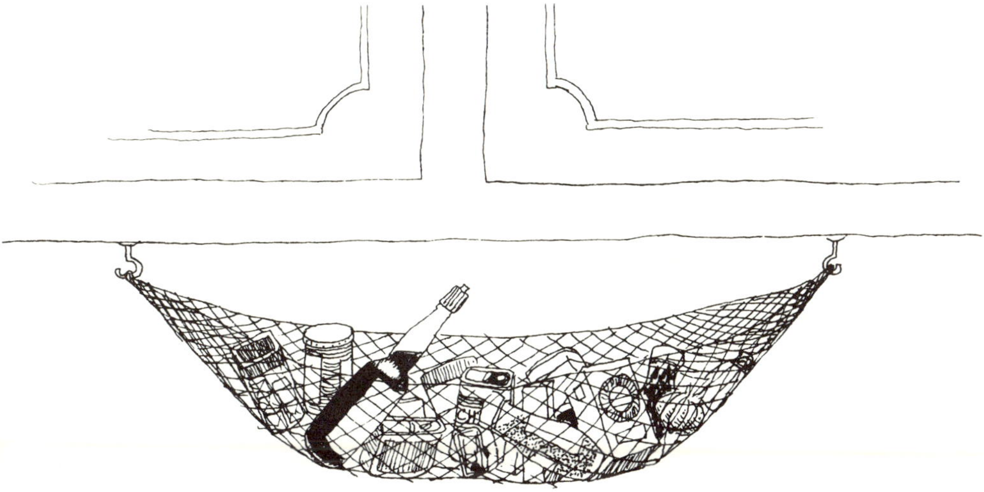

Chapter Eight
SAFETY AT SEA

Despite thirty-five-knot winds whipping up fifteen-foot swells, the thirty-footer rode like a cork, even making headway now and then. But there was no doubt that as rain clouds drove away the clear sky, it would be luck if we made it to port before dark. Over our shoulder Cape Finisterre, the notorious point marking the end of the Bay of Biscay, was already becoming invisibly wrapped in fog, and landmarks were disappearing. We dropped sail to the second reef points and fired up the engine, but with little effect. It was either come about and hope to make open water or find a tow, which, with the U. S. Coast Guard some 3,000 miles away, was far from a sure thing. Over the emergency channel we heard distress calls in four languages so, switching to a station used by local fishermen, we tried to raise one of the homebound trawlers and ask for a ride. Finally, we got help from a fine Portuguese crew, and made it to harbor. There, we barely had time to batten down before we were hit by a force niner with reported waves of eighty feet in the North Sea. Fifty-eight boats went down that night.

Looking back on that afternoon many times since, I have wondered what I would have done if the tow had not come through. Perhaps safety is not taken seriously until experience teaches the lesson of just how dangerous boating can be. However sobering this thought, keep it constantly in mind, and do everything possible to give your vessel a fighting chance. By the time you are in a situation to appreciate the need to take precautions, your life and the lives of all aboard may depend on them.

Though I am here concerned only with safety as it pertains to cooking, I have witnessed too many boating accidents not to offer some general advice. Regardless of the equipment aboard and the confidence you have in the Coast Guard, know your

Secured, yet instantly accessible, knives are safest in a wooden block.

own and the crew's and the vessel's limitations, keep a sharp eye on the weather, and remember that wisdom is the better part of valor. Safety is the most serious of all boating matters.

Just as the galley is a prime source of the crew's well-being, it is also a major source of hazards. Think first of steps that will safeguard the galley against mishaps; preventative measures are always better than curative measures. Secondly, do everything possible to make sure dangerous situations that do arise can be dealt with as quickly as possible.

Never forget that a galley may roll or pitch at any moment. The cook, working below and paying attention to his food, may not be able to anticipate the movement. Everything that a cook cannot hold in place with one hand, while using the other to hold himself in place, should be secured at all times. There should always be railed shelves with adequate empty space for this purpose.

Knives are safest in a block cut with slits and mounted within easy reach. Magnetic holders are not suited to boats; magnetic bars for holding knives will also offset the compass if it is within several feet, even if there is a fiberglass wall in between. Install hooks with clips so that the cook does not have to reach across the stove to get at them.

Gimbaled stoves are by far the safest, but they should be able to be locked into position for fueling. Fuel the stove carefully and clean up spills immediately. Top off the tank whenever the sea is calm, so there is no risk of running out during a meal or having to refuel in swells. Know your cooking fuel and make certain that a fire extinguisher, correct for that fuel, is placed between the stove and the nearest exit; check the pressure regularly. Routinely examine all fuel lines for leaks.

Even if the boat was purchased directly from a factory, keep an eye on the insulation around and above the stove. If it begins to buckle, or if adjacent bulkheads get more than warm, check it out completely. This goes double if there is an oven.

Matches are needed to start most stoves, but don't get the strike-anywhere variety; what you save in convenience is not worth the chance they will strike accidentally by rubbing together in a drawer. Waterproof matches are worth the extra expense, as anyone knows who has spent a futile half hour trying to strike the last box of wet matches. Battery-operated sparkers and old-fashioned flint strikers are better than matches for starting stoves because they do not use an open flame. However, matches should always be kept on board as a backup. If spent

Prevent eye-scorching flare-ups by always placing a pan on the burner before lighting the stove.

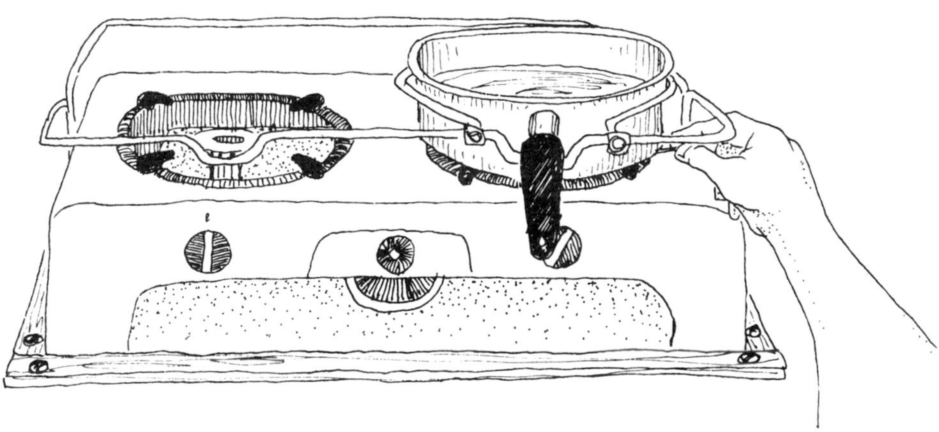

matches have a way of ending up all over the galley, a bean bag ashtray may help.

Never ignite a burner without a pot on top. In case of a flare-up, the flame will be partly contained by the pot instead of scorching the cabin roof or your eyebrows.

Store all liquors and other flammable liquids, such as cooking fuel, outside the galley and far from the stove. Paper towels are extremely flammable and should always be hung away from the stove. They are fine for cleaning, but become a hazard if used during cooking. Instead, hang a wipe towel within reach. It can be used to clean up spills during cooking, to wipe the cook's hands, and to remove hot grease before it burns.

If the hibachi is not a model that flips for dumping (the only type I recommend) or in case the fire gets out of control, attach a tether line so you won't have to think twice about tossing the whole thing overboard if necessary. Whenever a hibachi is used dockside, make certain the grill is on the leeward side of the vessel. This poses no problem on the hook as the stern is naturally downwind, but at the dock it is an extra precaution to remember.

Everyone knows to be careful of drinking water when traveling ashore, but people often forget that filling water tanks in a distant port can create the same problems. Often the distance from one state to another is enough. If the tanks do not hold enough water to make refilling unnecessary, carry purifying filters or water additives that are specially made for the purpose and available at most marine supply shops; "Topping them off" may have the same effect as refilling. When this is not possible, boil all water before drinking.

Examine the water tanks from time to time for leaks or other possible signs of contamination. Ideally, every vessel should have two independent tanks as a health precaution. This makes it possible to use the tank filled with local water for cooking and washing, while saving the water in the other tank for drinking.

Water consumption is the responsibility of the cook and should be measured, not just guessed at. If there is no guage to determine the water level, install one. It is every bit as important as measuring fuel. Crews use water at different rates, and only by keeping a constant eye on the supply can you make sure you don't run short.

A cook should always wear shoes in case a knife or something heavy falls off the counter. Cooking in a bathing suit is unwise, and a thick apron is necessary when in rough seas. Keep corrugated cardboard (it's thin and flat and takes up very little room) on hand to place on top of oil or other slippery spills until there is a chance to clean them up. Though under normal conditions glove potholders can be cumbersome, during storms the gloves are by far the best available because they give the firmest grip on a hot pot.

Keep an up-to-date supply of emergency provisions, adequate to feed the number of persons aboard for at least ten days. These supplies must be practical for life-raft conditions and should include a few basic utensils, a can opener and plenty of water. Keep all emergency provisions separate from the rest of the foods and where everyone aboard can get at them. Make certain that everyone knows where the emergency rations are kept. Include plenty of simple foods, including sea biscuit for calming stomachs.

Every galley should have a basic first aid kit geared to the galley. It should include eye wash, treatment for burns and cuts, tweezers and other basics.

Never leave sharp utensils lying around. Ice picks should always be stowed in a sheath. Try to find a ship's service that doesn't have sharp points. Blunted knives and forks work just as well as sharp ones and are far safer. Carry can openers that don't leave ragged edges or sheer off shards of metal which have to be fished out of the food.

Have a specific place for garbage, at hand, yet out of the way. The neater the galley the safer it is. Keep the sink clean and empty; it is one of the best places to drop a problem pot. Secure the soap. A built-in soap holder is a good idea; soap can be a slippery hazard as well as messy.

Keep an eye on drains and seacocks. A stray label from a can or jar can clog a pump, and a small problem can turn into a major catastrophe.

Most importantly, get to know your galley. Become as familiar as possible with it as quickly as you can. Learn where all the shutoffs are—fuel, electricity, overboard intakes for water. Know where lines go; you can't very well remove an olive pit that blocks the icebox drain if you don't know where the drain is and how to get at it. Don't rely on the captain or others in the crew to keep the galley running or bale you out in an emergency. Too often things go wrong all at once. The more self-sufficient each department is, the safer the vessel is bound to be. Even if assistance is only a few feet away, it may be some time before others can drop what they are doing to lend you a hand. Don't hesitate to shout for help when you need it, but do your level best to cope with problems yourself. If you are thoroughly familiar with the galley and its operation, and are well organized, you should at least be able to keep a problem from getting worse until help has time to arrive.

PART TWO The Steward's Recipes

The following recipes are arranged by meals—breakfast, lunch and dinner dishes—rather than in the traditional categories, such as vegetable, meat, fish and so forth. I feel this is a more useful system because boating meals must be planned ahead of time whereas meals on shore can, to some extent, be spur of the moment. If you are looking for a recipe for a particular food, look up the name of that food in the index.

Chapter Nine
BREAKFAST

PANMAN CAKES

1½ cups fresh fruit
2 cups milk
3 eggs
4 cups Bisquick
1 tablespoon jam
3 tablespoons butter
maple syrup
butter for topping

Dice fresh fruit and drain if necessary. Combine milk, eggs and Bisquick. Beat with a fork until smooth. Add fruit and jam; blend thoroughly. Heat a skillet, and add butter. Slowly pour batter by spoonful onto the skillet. Cook cakes on both sides until golden brown. Serve with syrup, or more jam, and butter.

Serves 6

COOKING AND PREP TIME: 20 minutes

RICED EGGS

1 cup uncooked brown rice
2 cups seawater
½ cup bacon bits, precooked ashore
salt and pepper
4 eggs

Combine rice, seawater, bacon bits, and salt and pepper to taste. Bring to a boil in a covered pot. Reduce heat and simmer for 40 minutes. Break eggs into the hot rice and stir until thoroughly mixed. Heat over low to medium heat, stirring gently until eggs have thickened.

Serves 4

COOKING AND PREP TIME: 50 minutes

SALSIFYING BREAKFAST

- 2 cups cut-up parsley
- 7 eggs, beaten
- 8 ounces mild Cheddar cheese, shredded
- 1/8 teaspoon lemon pepper
- salt
- 1 large onion, chopped
- 3 tablespoons butter
- 1 cup thin-sliced potatoes
- 1 cup thin-sliced salsify
- 2 tablespoons lemon juice
- 4 tablespoons lime juice

Combine parsley, eggs, cheese, lemon pepper and salt to taste, and set aside. Sauté onion in 1 tablespoon butter until soft. Steam potatoes and salsify in lemon and lime juice (a pressure cooker is ideal), until tender. Mash steamed vegetables, and add with sautéed onion to eggs. Heat remaining 2 tablespoons butter in a skillet. Pour egg mixture into skillet and cook until set and browned. Turn and brown on other side.

Serves 6

COOKING AND PREP TIME: 35 minutes

CURRIED MORNING MUSHROOMS

- 8 eggs, hard-cooked
- 2 tablespoons butter
- 1 garlic clove, minced
- 2 cups sliced scallions
- 2 cups sliced fresh mushrooms
- 1 teaspoon grated fresh gingerroot
- 1½ teaspoons curry powder
- 1 teaspoon sugar
- ½ teaspoon salt
- ¼ teaspoon pepper
- 2½ tablespoons flour
- 2 cups milk
- ½ cup sherry

Slice eggs and reserve. Heat butter in a skillet and add remaining ingredients except flour, milk and sherry. Simmer, stirring occasionally, for 5 minutes. Add flour and blend well. Add milk and sherry and stir until smooth and blended. Cook just below boiling until thickened. Gently lower egg slices into curry sauce and reheat; do not allow to boil.

Serves 6

COOKING AND PREP TIME: 15 minutes

ONE-EYE-OPEN OMELET

Candine, Grenada, West Indies

Break the general rule of always using an omelet pan and use your regular medium-size frying pan for this one.

- ½ teaspoon salt
- ⅓ cup milk
- 8 eggs, beaten
- 2 tablespoons butter
- 5 tablespoons wheat germ
- 1 cup whole-berry cranberry sauce

Add salt and milk to eggs and mix. Heat butter in a pan until foam starts to subside. Pour eggs into the pan and stir gently for 1 minute. Sprinkle on wheat germ and cranberry sauce. Cover and cook over low heat until berries are warm. With a spatula, carefully fold the omelet in half and serve family style.

Serves 4

COOKING AND PREP TIME: 15 minutes

CREAMED CHIPPED BEEF

Chugg, Essex, Connecticut

- 4 large potatoes
- 4 tablespoons butter
- 2 cups chipped beef
- 4 tablespoons flour
- 1½ cups milk
- ¼ cup beef broth (made with bouillon cube)
- ¼ cup sherry
- 3 tablespoons sour cream
- 1 teaspoon grated nutmeg
- salt and pepper

Peel potatoes and slice very thin. Cook potatoes in water to cover until tender, and drain. Melt 2 tablespoons butter in a pan. Add chipped beef and sauté for 2 minutes. Add remaining butter and melt. Add flour and stir until blended. Reduce heat. Add remaining ingredients except potatoes and seasoning, then cook over low heat, stirring, until blended and thickened. Add potatoes, nutmeg, and salt and pepper to taste. Heat, but do not boil. Serve when hot.

Serves 4

COOKING AND PREP TIME: 20 minutes

BREAKFAST DURING WINTER IN THE GULF

Shrimpdragger *Creole Lady*, Morehead City, N.C.

1 large onion, chopped
2 tablespoons butter
8 eggs, beaten
⅓ cup chopped green chilies
1 cup grated Cheddar cheese
3 large tomatoes, chopped
red cayenne
salt and pepper

Cook onion in butter until golden brown. Combine eggs with chilies, cheese and tomatoes, and season with cayenne, salt and pepper to taste; add to onion. Stir to mix thoroughly. Cook until set.

Serves 6

COOKING AND PREP TIME: 15 minutes

OATMEAL

2 cups oats
1 teaspoon salt
1 tablespoon honey
1 teaspoon ground cinnamon
2 cups orange juice
2 cups boiling water

Combine first 5 ingredients and stir into 2 cups boiling water. Bring to a boil and simmer for 5 to 10 minutes, depending upon consistency desired. Remove from heat and allow to cool, covered, for 5 minutes.

Serves 5

COOKING AND PREP TIME: 15 minutes

FOR VARIATIONS ADD:

¼ cup unsalted nuts, chopped fine and/or
½ cup raisins, and/or
½ cup cooked chopped prunes, and/or
½ tablespoon grated nutmeg

BLUE BREAKFAST

Schooner *Western Union*, Annapolis

- 4 pounds bluefish, filleted
- 3 eggs
- 2 tablespoons lemon juice
- salt and pepper
- 1½ cups flour
- 3 tablespoons butter, melted

Cut fish into 8 equal portions. Break eggs into a bowl. Add lemon juice and seasoning to taste to eggs. Dip fish into eggs, then roll in flour. Melt butter, 1 tablespoon at a time as needed, in a skillet and panfry fish, 1 or 2 pieces at a time. Turn to brown evenly.

Serves 8

COOKING AND PREP TIME: 25 minutes

SCRAMBLED EGGS AND MUSSELS

- 1 pound fresh mussels in shells
- 1 garlic clove, minced
- 1 bouillon cube (beef, chicken or vegetable)
- 2 tablespoons butter
- 1 cup chopped celery
- 1 cup chopped parsley
- 1 tablespoon soy sauce
- 1 tablespoon lemon juice
- 6 eggs, beaten
- salt and pepper

Scrub mussels and discard any not tightly shut. Heat ½ inch water in pot. Add garlic and bouillon cube. Add mussels, cover and simmer until all shells have opened. If one or two do not open, discard them. With tongs remove shells and drain. Heat butter in a large skillet. Add shelled mussels and remaining ingredients except eggs. Stir often. When hot, stir in eggs and cook until set.

Serves 6

COOKING AND PREP TIME: 30 minutes

BEATRICE A.

PANMAN EGG STRETCHER

Rebecca, Cape Breton Island, N.S.

6 slices of whole-grain bread
2 tablespoons butter
3 garlic cloves, minced
6 eggs, beaten
salt and pepper

Break bread into thumbnail-size pieces and panfry in butter and garlic until lightly browned. Add eggs and seasoning to taste, and cook until thickened.

Serves 6

COOKING AND PREP TIME: 15 minutes

CHEESE "GRILL"

Chugg, Essex, Connecticut

2½ tablespoons butter
2 slices of whole-wheat bread
1 thin slice of cooked ham
1 slice of American cheese
1 slice of tomato
1 thin slice of onion

Lightly butter both sides of bread slices. Pile remaining ingredients in between slices of bread. Melt remaining butter in a frying pan. Place sandwich in the pan and place a heavy dish or other weight on top. Cover and "grill" over low heat for 4 minutes. Turn and grill other side until cheese is melted and bread is golden brown.

Serves 1

COOKING AND PREP TIME: 6 minutes

NOTE: More than one sandwich may be grilled at a time.

Lunenburg, Nova Scotia, one of America's finest ports and home of the Schooner *Bluenose*.

PANCAKES POPEYE

½ pound spinach
4 tablespoons butter
1 cup milk
1 egg
2 cups flour
4 tablespoons baking powder
1 tablespoon honey
⅛ teaspoon ground allspice
2 tablespoons ground almonds

Wash spinach, cook, drain, and chop. While spinach is cooking, melt 3 tablespoons butter, cool, and combine with milk and egg in a bowl. Add flour, baking powder, honey and allspice, stirring slowly to blend. Add spinach and almonds and blend well. If batter is too thick, add more milk; if too thin, add more flour. Drop batter by spoonful onto a lightly buttered skillet. Cook pancakes until brown on both sides. Serve with jam, honey or maple syrup.

Serves 4 or 5

COOKING AND PREP TIME: 25 minutes

CHEESE AND VEGETABLE OMELET

Valkyrie, Rye, N.Y.

8 eggs, beaten
¼ cup milk
¼ teaspoon dried basil
½ cup grated Swiss or Cheddar cheese
¼ cup sliced fresh mushrooms
1 tomato, chopped
1 small onion, chopped
3 tablespoons butter
salt and pepper

Combine all ingredients except butter, adding salt and pepper to taste. Heat butter in a skillet over low heat. Add egg mixture, cover, and cook until eggs are firmly set, about 20 minutes. Quarter with a spatula and serve 1 wedge to a person.

Serves 4

COOKING AND PREP TIME: 30 minutes

EGGSTABLES

- 3 large sweet green peppers, chopped
- 4 large onions, sliced
- 3 tablespoons oil
- 1 cup thin-sliced zucchini
- 1 cup cooked beans, any kind
- 1 tablespoon vinegar
- ½ teaspoon dried thyme
- salt and pepper
- 6 eggs, beaten

Sauté peppers and onions in oil, stirring occasionally, until onions are transparent. Add zucchini, beans, vinegar, thyme, and seasoning to taste, and heat thoroughly. Add eggs and cook until eggs are creamy. Serve in a bowl.

Serves 6

COOKING AND PREP TIME: 20 minutes

FRENCH TOAST

- 4 eggs, beaten
- ½ cup milk
- salt and pepper
- 4 tablespoons butter
- 8 slices of bread
- 2 tablespoons fruit jam
- 1 teaspoon grated nutmeg
- 1 cup mashed berries

Combine eggs, milk, and salt and pepper to taste. Melt 2 tablespoons butter in a skillet. Dip bread, 1 slice at a time, into egg mixture. Fry in hot butter until golden brown on both sides. Top with fruit sauce.

FRUIT SAUCE:

Melt remaining 2 tablespoons butter in a saucepan. Add jam, nutmeg and mashed berries. Place over medium heat, stirring until blended and warm.

Serves 4

COOKING AND PREP TIME: 20 minutes

BUCKWHEAT CAKES

- 2 cups beer
- 3 cups buckwheat flour, approximately
- 3 tablespoons strawberry jam
- 1 cup chopped parsley
- salt and pepper
- 2 to 3 tablespoons butter

Blend first 4 ingredients in a bowl; batter should be slightly lumpy. Add salt and pepper to taste. Melt butter in a large pan. Pour off excess butter and save. Drop batter by spoonful into the hot, slightly buttered pan. Brown cakes on both sides. Add more of the butter as needed to cook the rest of the cakes. Serve hot with extra butter as a topping. Maple syrup is also excellent with these.

Serves 6

COOKING AND PREP TIME: 25 minutes

RARERAREBIT

- 2 tablespoons butter
- 2 eggs
- 1 cup baked beans, mashed
- 1 cup grated Cheddar cheese
- 1½ cups milk
- 1 teaspoon prepared mustard
- ½ cup bacon bits, precooked ashore
- 8 slices of whole-wheat toast

Heat butter in a skillet. Break eggs into hot butter. Immediately stir in baked beans. Add cheese, milk, mustard and bacon bits, stirring to blend. Cook until creamy. Spoon on top of toast.

Serves 4

COOKING AND PREP TIME: 25 minutes

DECK HAND'S SPECIAL

Chugg, Essex, Connecticut

- 4 large potatoes
- 2 tablespoons butter
- 2 cups chipped beef
- 1 large onion, chopped
- ½ cup chopped parsley
- salt and pepper
- 2 eggs

Peel and dice potatoes. Boil potatoes in water to cover for approximately 20 minutes. Melt butter in a pan and heat until steaming. Add beef and sauté for 2 minutes. Add onion, parsley, and seasoning to taste. Sauté for 4 minutes, stirring occasionally. Add eggs, stir to combine, and cook until set, about 5 minutes.

Serves 4

COOKING AND PREP TIME: 30 minutes

Chapter Ten
LUNCH

STEWARD'S SALAD

Schooner *Bill of Rights*, Newport

- ½ head of lettuce, torn into bite-sized pieces
- 1 large cucumber, peeled or scrubbed, sliced thin
- 1 can (7¾ ounces) salmon, drained
- 1 can (3¾ ounces) skinned and boned sardines
- 2 cups cold cooked peas
- 1 cup cold cooked broccoli
- ½ cup black olives, drained

Combine ingredients and toss with Sea Chef's Dressing (p. 117).

Serves 4

COOKING AND PREP TIME: 10 minutes

MOLASSES HAM SANDWICH

- 2 tablespoons molasses
- ½ tablespoon prepared mustard
- ½ cup raisins
- ¼ tablespoon ground cinnamon
- ½ cup orange juice
- 6 thick slices of cooked or smoked ham
- 6 slices of bread

Combine molasses, mustard, raisins, cinnamon and orange juice. Place over low heat, and stir to blend. Place ham on bread and spoon on hot sauce.

Serves 6

COOKING AND PREP TIME: 10 minutes

LENTIL BURGERS

Hineronji, Pool, Yorkshire, England

This was given to me by a family of five cruising the world aboard a 40-foot sloop.

- 1 large onion, cut up
- 2 tablespoons butter
- 2 garlic cloves, minced
- salt and pepper
- 4 cups cooked lentils
- 1 cup chopped mushrooms
- 1 tablespoon safflower oil

Sauté onion in butter with garlic and seasoning to taste. Combine lentils, mushrooms and sautéed onion and mash into a paste. Form paste into patties. Heat oil in a skillet and sauté burgers, browning both sides. Serve between slices of bread; rye is best.

Serves 4

COOKING AND PREP TIME: 20 minutes

SEA CHEF'S SALAD NUMBER ONE

- 1 avocado, peeled and cut up
- 2 pimientos, sliced
- ½ cup sliced mushrooms
- ½ head of lettuce, in bite-size pieces
- ½ cup shredded mild Cheddar cheese
- ¼ cup grated Parmesan cheese
- 2 tablespoons crumbled blue cheese
- 1 can (7¾ ounces) water-packed tuna
- ¼ teaspoon dry mustard
- 3 tablespoons vinegar
- 1 teaspoon garlic salt
- ¼ teaspoon dried basil
- salt and pepper
- 2 tablespoons safflower oil

Combine vegetables, cheeses and tuna in a large bowl. Dissolve mustard in vinegar and add garlic salt, basil, and seasoning to taste. Mix with oil, and pour over salad. Toss thoroughly and serve with chunks of bread.

Serves 4

COOKING AND PREP TIME: 15 minutes

PANCAKE SANDWICH

- 3 cups Bisquick
- 1¾ cups milk
- 3 eggs
- 3 tablespoons butter
- 8 ounces canned ham spread (or liver or chicken, etc.)
- 1 tablespoon pineapple juice
- 2 celery ribs, diced
- salt and pepper

Blend Bisquick, milk and eggs with a fork until creamy. Grease a skillet with butter and heat until very hot. Pour batter by spoonfuls into skillet. Brown until golden on both sides. Allow cakes to cool. Mix ham spread with pineapple juice and diced celery. Season to taste. Spread onto pancakes and serve. This is excellent with soup.

Serves 5

COOKING AND PREP TIME: 20 minutes

CHEF'S SALAD

The first time I served this meal the crew laughed and said I had finally gone off the deep end, serving a "salad" instead of "real food" for lunch. To their surprise and my satisfaction, they ate both the salad and their words. It soon became an asked-for favorite.

- ½ head of lettuce, torn into bite-sized pieces
- 3 large tomatoes, cut in eighths
- 1 large cucumber, sliced thin
- 4 water-packed artichoke hearts, drained and quartered
- ½ cup green olives with pimiento stuffing, chopped
- 3 scallions, chopped small
- ½ pound Lebanon bologna, cut into small pieces
- 1½ cups cut-up cooked chicken or turkey
- 1½ cups diced cooked ham
- 2 cups cut-up cauliflower, raw or cooked
- 2 tablespoons chopped parsley

Combine all ingredients, toss, and serve with Sea Chef's Dressing (p. 117).

Serves 4

COOKING AND PREP TIME: 10 minutes

The *Bill of Rights* (right) at its mooring in Newport, Rhode Island.

WINDSONG'S EGG AND BEAN-SPROUT SANDWICH

Schooner *Windsong*, Cook Islands

- 6 eggs
- 2 cups bean sprouts, chopped*
- ¼ cup chopped walnuts
- 2 tablespoons butter
- 8 slices of whole-wheat bread
- 4 ounces cream cheese

Combine eggs with bean sprouts and walnuts, and scramble in butter. On each of 4 slices of bread, spread cream cheese. Add egg mixture. Top with remaining bread slices. If weather is cool, serve with soup; it heats while sandwiches are being prepared.

Serves 4

COOKING AND PREP TIME: 20 minutes

* HINT: Bring mung beans and grow your own sprouts. They take only a couple of days, and need very little room.

BEAN-SPROUT SANDWICH

- 8 slices of oatmeal bread
- 1 onion, chopped
- 4 tablespoons vinegar
- 2 tablespoons prepared mustard
- 8 pitted black olives, cut up
- 8 slices of American cheese
- 4 pimientos, split into halves
- 2 cups bean sprouts
- salt and pepper

Toast bread slightly. Cook onion in vinegar and mustard until onion is translucent. Add olives and cook until hot. Drain. On each of 4 slices of bread, place, in this order, 1 piece of cheese, 1 pimiento spread out flat, ½ cup bean sprouts, some onion and olive mixture and 1 slice of cheese. Season to taste. Top with another slice of bread and serve.

Serves 4

COOKING AND PREP TIME: 15 minutes

COURTESAN'S CREAMED VEGETABLES

Courtesan, West Islip, New York

- 2 cups chopped fresh Brussels sprouts
- 2 cups thin slices of peeled yams
- 1 cup strips of carrots
- 1 cup cut-up celery
- 2 cups unsalted raw peanuts
- ¼ cup shredded Mozzarella cheese
- ½ cup dry vermouth
- 6 tablespoons butter
- 6 tablespoons flour
- 3 cups milk
- 1 slice of gingerroot
- salt and pepper

Steam vegetables and peanuts in a pressure cooker. Drain and reserve vegetables. Combine cheese, vermouth and butter in a pan. Place over low heat, and stir until blended. Slowly add flour, stirring until creamy. Blend in milk and heat, but do not boil. Add gingerroot, and seasoning to taste. When sauce is hot, serve over the steamed vegetables.

Serves 6

COOKING AND PREP TIME: 25 minutes

KARL'S DELIGHT

Aimless, Annapolis

- ½ cup chipped beef
- 1 cup uncooked shelled peas
- 2 tomatoes, chopped
- 2 tablespoons butter
- 2 cups uncooked elbow macaroni
- 1 cup shredded Cheddar cheese
- 3 carrots, cut into sticks

Cook beef, peas and tomatoes in butter for 7 minutes. Stir occasionally. Cook macaroni in water until done to your taste, and drain. Add macaroni to beef mixture. Add cheese and mix with a spoon over low heat. Serve when the cheese melts and thickens the mixture. Serve with carrot sticks.

Serves 3

COOKING AND PREP TIME: 25 minutes

THIN SPAGHETTI WITH THICK SAUCE

- 4 tomatoes, peeled, seeded, and cut up
- 2 cups cooked black beans, chopped
- ½ pound zucchini, cut up small
- 4 tablespoons tomato paste
- 1 cup water
- 2 tablespoons Worcestershire sauce
- 1 garlic clove, minced
- 1 teaspoon celery salt
- 1 teaspoon lemon pepper
- salt and pepper
- 1 pound thin spaghetti

Combine vegetables and tomato paste with 1 cup water. Add Worcestershire, garlic, celery salt and lemon pepper. Cook over medium heat, stirring occasionally to blend, for 30 minutes. Season to taste. While sauce is cooking, cook spaghetti; it may be boiled in seawater. When done to your taste, drain. Serve sauce over spaghetti.

Serves 5

COOKING AND PREP TIME: 40 minutes

AVOCADO ACAPULCO

VBC, Loch Arbour, New Jersey

- 2 avocados, peeled and pitted
- 2 tomatoes, chopped
- 2 scallions, chopped
- 2 sweet bell peppers, seeded and diced
- 2 tablespoons lemon juice
- ¼ teaspoon chili powder
- cayenne
- 8 soft tortillas
- 8 slices of Muenster cheese

Combine avocados, tomatoes, scallions, peppers, lemon juice, chili powder and cayenne to taste. Spoon some on top of each tortilla and top with a slice of cheese.

Serves 4

COOKING AND PREP TIME: 15 minutes

PEA SOUP THICK AS A FOG

- 1 pound split peas (unless instant variety, must be pre-soaked)
- 4 quarts beef broth (made from bouillon cubes)
- 3 potatoes, peeled and diced
- ½ head of cabbage, shredded
- 3 cups diced ham
- ¼ cup dry red wine
- ¼ cup dry vermouth
- 2 tablespoons dry mustard
- 1 teaspoon black pepper
- salt

Combine all ingredients except salt in a pressure cooker and cook over low heat for 45 minutes. Add salt to taste. Serve with chunks of thick bread.

Serves 10

COOKING AND PREP TIME: 55 minutes

BOILED POTATOES AUGMENTED

- 2 cups shelled fresh peas
- 6 large potatoes, peeled, cut into large pieces
- 1 cup vinegar
- 1 tablespoon butter
- ¼ pound Cheddar cheese shredded
- 1 garlic clove, minced
- ½ teaspoon dried thyme

Boil peas in water to cover for 4 minutes. Boil potatoes in water to cover until tender. While potatoes are boiling, combine peas with remaining ingredients and heat until cheese has melted. Stir to blend. Spoon over drained potatoes.

Serves 4

COOKING AND PREP TIME: 25 minutes

SAVORY ZUCCHINI

Schooner *Bill of Rights*, Newport

The captain's favorite dish.

- 3 large zucchini, sliced thin
- ½ cup vinegar
- 3 tablespoons butter
- salt
- ½ cup thin slices of Cheddar cheese or grated Parmesan

Combine zucchini, vinegar and butter in a large skillet. Cover and simmer for 10 minutes. Add salt to taste. Sprinkle with cheese, cover, and cook until cheese is melted. Serve as is, over whole-grain bread, or as a side dish.

Serves 4

COOKING AND PREP TIME: 20 minutes

Bound away aboard the *Bill of Rights*.

GREEN BEAN "CASSEROLE"

- 1 large onion, cut up
- 2 tablespoons butter
- 2 tablespoons flour
- 1 cup milk
- ¾ pound fresh green beans
- 2 sweet green peppers, seeded and cut up
- 1½ cups mushrooms, sliced thin
- 1 cup almonds, chopped
- ¼ pound mozzarella, sliced thin
- 1 tablespoon paprika

Sauté onion in butter until golden. Blend in flour. Add milk; stir and cook over low heat until sauce is creamy. Set aside. Boil beans in water to cover until tender; drain. Combine beans, peppers, mushrooms and almonds, and add to onion sauce in pot. Cover and cook, but do not boil, over low heat for 10 minutes. Top with cheese. When cheese melts, sprinkle with paprika and serve at once.

Serves 3 or 4

COOKING AND PREP TIME: 20 minutes

KAPUCIJNERS

Bylgia, The Netherlands

The soloist who gave me this recipe was a prospector in North Africa before he became a round-the-world sailor. He starts out with about 80 percent of the supplies he will need for the 2-year voyage. Most of his diet consists of natural foods which he has specially packaged so that they will keep without spoiling or loss of nutritional value.

- 3 cups shelled peas
- 3 cups uncooked brown rice
- 6 cups water
- 3 large onions, chopped
- 2 garlic cloves, minced
- 2 tablespoons butter
- 1 cup cooked soybeans
- ½ cup raisins
- 3 cups cooked brown beans

If peas are dried, soak them in water overnight. Cook peas and rice together in approximately 6 cups of water for 50 minutes. Sauté onions and garlic in butter. Mash soybeans, raisins and brown beans into a paste. Combine with peas, rice and onions.

Serves 7

COOKING AND PREP TIME: 55 minutes

ORIENTAL CHICKEN

- 2 to 3 tablespoons safflower oil
- 1 cup diced mushrooms
- 1½ pounds canned boned chicken, diced
- ½ cup chopped canned ham
- 1½ cups cooked peas
- 2 cups bean sprouts
- 1 cup canned or fresh pineapple, cut into squares
- 2 tablespoons soy sauce
- 1 teaspoon brown sugar
- 1 teaspoon ground ginger

Heat 2 tablespoons oil in a wok. Add mushrooms, diced chicken and ham, and the peas. Stir-fry quickly for 1 or 2 minutes. Remove vegetables and meat from wok and set aside in a covered dish. Add more oil to the wok if necessary, and stir-fry bean sprouts and pineapple. Add soy sauce, brown sugar and ginger. Stir to dissolve sugar. Heat until bean-sprout mixture is steaming, then add mushroom-chicken mixture. Cover and cook for 3 minutes. Serve with rice if desired (although for me it stands well enough alone).

Serves 5

COOKING AND PREP TIME: 10 minutes

EGG AND TOMATO

- 3 tomatoes, cut in eighths
- 6 water chestnuts, chopped
- 4 eggs, beaten
- ¼ tablespoon lemon pepper
- 1 tablespoon oil
- 2 tablespoons grated coconut
- 1 tablespoon soy sauce
- 1 teaspoon sugar
- 1 teaspoon dried marjoram
- salt

Combine eggs, water chestnuts and lemon pepper; set aside. Heat oil in a wok. Add tomato wedges and stir briskly for 10 seconds. Add coconut, soy sauce, sugar, marjoram, and salt to taste. Heat while stirring for 2 minutes. Pour in egg mixture, and gently scramble until eggs have set to desired firmness.

Serves 4

COOKING AND PREP TIME: 10 minutes

STIR-FRIED SARDINES

- 1 pound thin spaghetti
- 2 tablespoons olive oil
- ¼ pound fresh spinach, torn into bite sized pieces
- 4 tablespoons tomato paste
- 3 tablespoons vinegar
- 1 can (3¾ ounces) boneless sardines, drained
- ¾ cup pimientos, cut up
- 3 large scallions, sliced thin
- 4 tablespoons soy sauce
- 3 slices of gingerroot, minced
- 1 teaspoon brown sugar
- salt and pepper

Cook spaghetti in seawater until done *al dente*, about 15 minutes. Meanwhile heat 1 tablespoon oil in a wok and stir-fry spinach. Remove spinach to a small bowl. Blend tomato paste with vinegar and combine with sardines, pimientos, scallions and soy sauce. Heat remaining oil in the wok and stir-fry gingerroot. Add spinach and sardine mixture. Stir in brown sugar, and salt and pepper to taste. While stirring, heat until very hot. Serve on top of spaghetti.

Serves 4

COOKING AND PREP TIME: 25 minutes

SALMON STIR-FRY

- 2 beef bouillon cubes
- 4½ cups seawater, boiling
- 2 cups uncooked brown rice
- 3 tablespoons olive oil
- 1 small eggplant, diced
- 1½ cups frozen baby lima beans
- 1 can (7¾ ounces) salmon
- 1 large red onion, chopped
- 4 tablespoons sherry
- 3 tablespoons soy sauce
- 1 teaspoon dried thyme
- 1 tablespoon garlic powder
- salt and pepper

Dissolve bouillon cubes in the 4½ cups boiling seawater. Bring to a second boil. Add rice, cover, and simmer until done. When rice is nearly cooked, heat 2 tablespoons oil in a wok, until almost smoking. Stir-fry eggplant and lima beans. Set aside in a covered dish. Add remaining oil if necessary and stir-fry salmon and red onion for 2 minutes. Add sherry, soy sauce, thyme, garlic powder and stir-fried vegetables. Cover and cook until all ingredients are hot. Season with salt and pepper to taste. Serve over rice.

Serves 3 or 4

COOKING AND PREP TIME: 30 minutes

SAILOR'S VEGETABLE SUKIYAKI

- 2 to 3 tablespoons soy oil
- 2 slices of gingerroot, minced
- 2 cucumbers, sliced thin
- 3 apples, cored, peeled and cut up
- 1 sweet green pepper, salted and cut into strips
- ¼ cup chopped chives
- 1½ cups sliced mushrooms
- 1 pound fresh kale, in bite-sized pieces
- 4 scallions, chopped
- ½ cup soy sauce
- ¼ cup honey
- ¼ cup sherry
- 2 garlic cloves, minced
- ½ teaspoon dry mustard
- 2 cups bean sprouts
- salt

Heat 2 to 3 tablespoons oil in a wok. Stir-fry gingerroot, cucumbers, apples, green pepper, chives, mushrooms, kale and scallions. Remove vegetables to a covered dish. Combine remaining ingredients except bean sprouts in the wok. Add bean sprouts and other vegetables when hot. Add salt to taste. Cover and cook over very low heat for 5 minutes. Serve with rice or thin spaghetti.

Serves 4

COOKING AND PREP TIME: 20 minutes

Chapter Eleven
DINNER

CHAPATI

An easy and useful recipe. *Chapatis* takes the place of bread, tortillas, rolls and buns.

- 1 pound whole-wheat flour
- 3 tablespoons oil
- ¼ to ½ cup lukewarm water
- flour for rolling
- oil for cooking

Mix flour and oil together in a bowl or on a board. Add water to flour, 1 tablespoon at a time, working it around with your hands. Keep adding water until you have a stiff dough. Rinse, dry, and oil your hands, and knead the dough for about 5 minutes. Cover the dough with a damp towel and let it rest for 30 minutes.

Take a lump of dough about the size of a lime and roll it between the palms to make a ball as wide across as the size of a handball. Flatten out to about 1 inch thick. Dip into flour and roll out on a board or counter. The trick in rolling is to keep a very light touch. Roll from the center toward the outside to form a thin round of dough, like a medium-size pancake. Do not let the center get thinner than the edges. As you roll, keep lifting and turning over the dough, adding flour to the board or your hands, if necessary.

Lightly oil a skillet or griddle, as for pancakes. When very hot, drop in one *chapati*, cook briefly until it reaches a medium tan color, 1 to 2 minutes, then turn and tan the other side. Set aside on a plate. While one *chapati* is cooking, you can roll out the next one. Add oil to the skillet as needed, but not too much, and be sure to let any added oil get very hot before dropping in the *chapati*.

Makes about 12

STROGANOFF SHAZAAM

Shazaam, Marblehead

- 2½ cups uncooked noodles
- 2 pounds chuck steak, cubed
- 6 tablespoons flour
- 2 tablespoons sesame oil
- 2 large onions, chopped
- ½ cup water
- ½ cup sherry
- 2½ cups uncooked shelled peas
- 2 pints sour cream
- 2 cups beef broth (made from bouillon cubes)
- salt and pepper

Boil noodles in water to cover until done to your taste. Dredge beef with 3 tablespoons flour. Heat oil in a deep skillet and brown beef. Add onions and cook until brown. Blend in remaining flour and ½ cup water. Add sherry and peas. Cover and cook over low heat, stirring occasionally, for 10 minutes. Stir in sour cream and beef broth, cover, and heat (do not boil), stirring often, for another 10 minutes. Season to taste. Serve stew over noodles.

Serves 4

COOKING AND PREP TIME: 40 minutes

LABSKAUS

Segelschulschiff Gorch Fock, Kiel, West Germany

- 1 pound pork, cut up
- 1 pound beef, cut up
- 5 carrots, cut up
- 1 bunch of celery, cut up
- 3 beets, peeled and sliced
- 2 cucumbers, peeled and sliced thick
- 2 large onions, cut up
- 3 garlic cloves, minced
- 4 leeks, cut up
- ½ cup bacon bits, precooked ashore
- 2 tablespoons butter
- salt and pepper

Steam pork and beef in very little water until almost tender. Add carrots, celery, beets and cucumbers and cook until all the vegetables are tender. Add beef, pork and vegetable mixture to the onion mixture with seasoning to taste. Cover, heat for 3 minutes, and serve. May be served with fried eggs.

Serves 8

COOKING AND PREP TIME: 50 minutes

The *Gorch Fock* bound out of Lisbon.

NOGO BAY VEGETABLES

Somora, Okinawa

- 2 ounces soy sauce
- 1 teaspoon prepared mustard
- 2 ounces sherry
- 4 chicken breasts, deboned and sliced
- 1 medium-size rutabaga, shredded with potato peeler
- 5 carrots, cut into strips
- 1 small onion, sliced thin
- 2 tablespoons oil
- salt and pepper

Blend soy sauce, mustard and sherry, and set aside. Stir-fry chicken and vegetables in the oil in a wok. Add soy sauce mixture and reheat. Season to taste. Serve.

Serves 4

COOKING AND PREP TIME: 15 minutes

ERBSENEINTOPF

Segelschulschiff Gorch Fock, Kiel, West Germany

- 3 large potatoes, scrubbed, large dice
- 1 cup uncooked shelled peas
- 1 cup long thin slices of carrot
- 4 celery ribs, cut up
- 2 large onions, cut up
- 3 leeks, cut up
- 1 cup bacon bits, precooked ashore
- ½ pound salt pork
- 3 tablespoons butter
- 1 pound bockwurst
- ½ pound mettwurst
- 1 tablespoon dried marjoram
- ¼ cup water
- salt and pepper

Boil potatoes, peas, carrots and celery in water to cover until tender. Sauté onions, leeks, bacon bits and salt pork in butter until onions have browned. Drain boiled vegetables and add to onion mixture. Add remaining meats, the marjoram, ¼ cup water, and salt and pepper to taste. Cover and cook over low heat for 20 minutes. Serve.

Serves 8

COOKING AND PREP TIME: 55 minutes

STEAMED CLAMS

Dig for steamer clams at low tide (away from harbors or other waters liable to be contaminated) by stomping on the sand near the waterline; there should be small air holes made by the clams. When a spray of water shoots up near your foot, dig down quickly until you reach the clam. It takes a little practice to catch the clams (adept diggers themselves) without breaking their shells, which makes them too sandy to use.

- 3 quarts freshly dug steamers
- 4 potatoes, peeled and sliced very thin
- 3 scallions, cut up
- 3 tablespoons butter
- ½ cup soy sauce
- ½ cup seawater
- ½ cup lemon juice

Soak live steamers in seawater for 40 minutes to purge sand. Brown potatoes and scallions in butter in a skillet. Steam clams in soy sauce, ½ cup seawater and lemon juice until shells open, about 7 minutes. Serve with browned potatoes.

Serves 4

COOKING AND PREP TIME: 1 hour

STEAMED CELERY AND FISH

Chugg, Essex, Connecticut

- 8 celery ribs, cut into 3 inch pieces
- 1 lemon, cut in eighths
- 2 bay leaves
- 2 garlic cloves, minced
- 2 pounds fish, filleted
- 2 tablespoons butter
- 2 tablespoons lemon juice
- salt

Steam celery together with lemon slices, bay leaves, and garlic in a covered shallow pan until celery is tender. Panbroil fish in butter and lemon juice. Season fish with salt to taste. Spoon celery over fish and serve. (Extra juice may be spooned over potatoes, vegetables or fresh salad.)

Serves 4

COOKING AND PREP TIME: 20 minutes

Rhode Island sunset on the eve of a Nor'easter.

RICE PILAF

Northern Cross, Newport

- 4 chicken bouillon cubes
- 3½ cups hot water
- 2 cups uncooked brown rice
- 1 cup chopped mushrooms
- 1 onion, diced
- 2 tablespoons butter

Dissolve bouillon cubes in 3½ cups water. Add rice and bring to a boil. Reduce heat and simmer for 20 minutes. Add mushrooms and onion. Stir gently. Cover and simmer for another 20 minutes. Stir in butter. This is delicious with panbroiled ham.

Serves 4

COOKING AND PREP TIME: 45 minutes

CALAMARES

Pinta, Bayona, Spain

- 2 pounds fresh squid, cleaned and sliced (remove skin if you like)
- ½ cup fine bread crumbs
- 6 ounces butter, melted
- ½ cup sherry

Mix bread crumbs with ¼ cup melted butter and turn squid pieces in the mixture until well coated. Pan-fry squid in remaining melted butter for 4 minutes. Add sherry, cover, and cook over low heat for 2 minutes. Serve with the cooking mixture spooned over.

Serves 4

COOKING AND PREP TIME: 15 minutes

NAVY BEANS CIVILIAN STYLE

1 chicken bouillon cube
5 cups water
3 cups dried navy beans, soaked in water overnight
1 cup corn kernels
2 cups cut-up zucchini
¼ pound salt pork, cut up
¼ cup dry vermouth

Dissolve bouillon cube in 1 cup of the water, boiling. Combine all ingredients with remaining 4 cups water in a pot. Bring to a boil, then simmer over low heat, stirring occasionally, for 45 minutes.

Serves 5

COOKING AND PREP TIME: 1 hour

CHICKEN IN A POT

Obsession, Westport, Connecticut

2 cups uncooked elbow macaroni
3 cups fresh water
½ cup dry white wine
1½ pounds boned chicken (canned is fine)
6 ounces tomato paste
1 red onion, minced
2 tablespoons butter
½ cup lime juice
½ cup grated Cheddar cheese
1 teaspoon garlic salt
½ teaspoon dried tarragon
¼ teaspoon pepper
salt

Boil macaroni in seawater until about half-done. Drain, then add 2½ cups *fresh* water, the wine and chicken. Mix tomato paste with remaining ½ cup fresh water. Steam onion in butter, tomato-paste mixture and lime juice. Add cheese, garlic salt, tarragon and pepper, and combine with chicken and macaroni. Simmer over medium-low heat for 20 minutes. Add salt to taste. Serve in bowls.

Serves 5

COOKING AND PREP TIME: 1 hour

SPAGHETTI WITH MUSSELS

- 2 pounds fresh mussels in shells
- 1 pound spinach spaghetti
- 1½ cups fresh water
- salt
- 2 tablespoons butter
- 2 tablespoons oil
- 1 garlic clove, minced
- 2 tomatoes, cut into quarters
- 2 celery ribs, diced
- 12 ounces tomato paste
- 1 teaspoon dried orégano

Scrub mussels and remove beards. Discard any with open shells. Boil spaghetti in water to cover until cooled *al dente*. While spaghetti is cooking, steam mussels in 1½ cups lightly salted water. Remove mussels from shells, discarding any that have not opened. Strain the mussel liquor and set aside. Melt butter with oil in a saucepan, and add garlic, tomatoes and diced celery. Cook for a few minutes, then add tomato paste and orégano. Cover and simmer, stirring often, for 30 minutes. Stir mussels into the sauce with enough of the strained mussel liquor to give the right consistency. Toss with spaghetti and serve very hot.

Serves 5

COOKING AND PREP TIME: 45 minutes

SEA BASS OR GROUPER

- 1 cup lime juice
- ¼ cup vinegar
- 4 pound grouper or sea bass, filleted
- 1 sweet green pepper, seeded and cut up
- 1 lime, sliced thin
- ½ cup cracker crumbs
- 1 tablespoon chili powder

Mix lime juice and vinegar. Marinate fish fillets in the mixture for 45 minutes. Remove ribs and seeds from pepper and cut into pieces. Combine fish and marinade with remaining ingredients, and simmer in a covered skillet for 15 minutes. Serve with rice or vegetables.

Serves 8

COOKING AND PREP TIME: 65 minutes

MEAT AND POTATOES PLUS

6 potatoes, peeled and sliced thick
1 pound lean beef, cut into bite-sized pieces
1 medium-size onion, chopped
½ pound sausage, sliced
2 tablespoons butter
2 tablespoons olive oil
2 cups fresh water
2 zucchini, sliced
1 small eggplant, sliced thick
6 ounces tomato paste
salt and pepper

Place potatoes in a pot and cover with water. Boil for 20 minutes, or until done. Sauté beef, onion and sausage in butter and oil, stirring, for 7 minutes. Drain potatoes. Add 2 cups fresh water and meat mixture to potatoes. Add vegetables, tomato paste, and salt and pepper to taste. Bring to a boil, stirring gently to blend. Cover and simmer for 5 minutes.

Serves 4

COOKING AND PREP TIME: 40 minutes

BLUES, BASS OR FLOUNDER FRY

Marjorie Ellen, Rowayton, Connecticut

2 large fish fillets
½ cup white wine
¼ cup lime juice
¼ cup vinegar
5 tablespoons butter
3 tablespoons flour
1½ cups milk
½ cup sliced mushrooms
¼ cup slivered blanched almonds
salt and pepper

Marinate fish fillets in a mixture of wine, lime juice and vinegar for at least 45 minutes. Drain, but reserve the marinade. Melt 3 tablespoons butter in a pan. Add flour and stir until blended. Add milk and ¼ cup of the reserved marinade. Place over medium heat, but do not boil, and stir until creamy. Add mushrooms and almonds. Season with salt and pepper to taste. Melt remaining 2 tablespoons butter in a skillet. Panfry fish in butter until both sides are golden. Pour mushroom and almond sauce over fish. Reheat and serve.

Serves 6

COOKING AND PREP TIME: 1 hour

OYSTERS DELMARVA

- 2½ dozen oysters in shells
- 3 tablespoons melted butter
- 1 cup chopped parsley
- 2 tablespoons vinegar
- 2 tablespoons garlic salt
- ¼ teaspoon dried tarragon
- lemon pepper

Scrub oysters, and steam in about 2 inches of water until shells open. Remove oysters from steamer and strain broth through a fine sieve or cheesecloth. Remove oysters from shells and combine with 1 tablespoon butter, the parsley, vinegar, garlic salt, tarragon, and lemon pepper to taste, in a large saucepan. Add ½ cup strained oyster broth and remaining melted butter. Stir. Cover and place over very low heat for 5 minutes. Serve with pasta.

Serves 5

COOKING AND PREP TIME: 30 minutes

GARDEN CURRY

- 2 cups uncooked brown rice
- 1 large yellow onion, minced
- 1 red onion, minced
- 2 celery ribs, chopped
- 3 garlic cloves, minced
- 3 scallions, sliced thin
- 3 tablespoons butter
- 2 tablespoons curry powder
- 3 tablespoons flour
- 1 cup cooked chick-peas
- 1 cup cooked peas
- ½ pound mushrooms, sliced
- ½ cup lemon juice
- ¼ cup dry sherry
- 2 pints sour cream
- salt and pepper
- hot sauce

Stir rice into 4½ cups boiling water (seawater is fine). Cover and bring to a boil. Reduce heat and simmer, covered, for 40 minutes, or until rice is done. Meanwhile, sauté onions, celery, garlic and scallions in butter until onions are transparent. Add curry powder and cook and stir for 2 minutes. Add flour, mix well, then add vegetables, lemon juice and sherry. Heat and mix. Stir in sour cream, then add seasoning and hot sauce to taste. Heat but do not boil. Serve over rice.

Serves 4 or 5

COOKING AND PREP TIME: 50 minutes

CHIVE MUSSELS

Aimless, Annapolis, Maryland

This is a meal you can gather yourself almost anywhere at low tide. In 15 minutes you'll have enough to feed 15 hungry diners. Just make sure you gather mussels outside boat basins and other possibly polluted areas. Also, pick only mussels that are still under water and make sure shells are closed.

- 2 cups uncooked rice
- 4 pounds fresh mussels in shells
- 1 pound boned chicken, cut in small pieces
- 3 tablespoons oil
- 4 cups chopped chives
- 2 cups shelled fresh peas
- ¼ pound sausage, sliced
- 4 pimientos, cut up
- 3 tomatoes, peeled and cut up
- ¼ cup soy sauce
- ½ cup cornstarch
- ¼ cup cold water
- 1 tablespoon honey
- salt and pepper

Cook rice in water until done to your taste. Scrub mussels and remove beards. Discard any shells that are not tightly closed. Steam mussels in a large covered pot until shells open, about 7 minutes. Remove mussels from shells and set aside. Cut chicken into small pieces. Heat oil in a wok. Add chives, chicken, peas, sausage and pimientos, and stir-fry. Add tomatoes and soy sauce. Stir in cornstarch, blended with ¼ cup water. Add honey and seasoning to taste. Cover and cook over low heat, stirring occasionally, until thickened. Gently stir in shelled mussels and just heat. Serve with rice.

Serves 8

COOKING AND PREP TIME: 35 minutes

FRESH MUSSEL MEAL

- 2 cups uncooked rice
- 2 pounds fresh mussels in shells
- 2 large onions, sliced
- 3 tomatoes, chopped
- 3 tablespoons butter
- ½ lemon, sliced thin
- salt and pepper

Cook rice until done to your taste. Scrub mussels and remove beards. Steam mussels until shells open. Remove mussels from shells. Strain steaming liquid through a fine sieve or cheesecloth. Sauté onions and tomatoes in butter until onions are translucent. Add cooked rice, mussels with ½ cup strained hot mussel broth, and lemon slices. Simmer covered stirring occasionally, for 10 minutes. Season to taste.

Serves 4

COOKING AND PREP TIME: 40 minutes

RHODE ISLAND LAMB STEW

Schooner *Bill of Rights*, Newport

- 2 large onions, cut up
- 2 cups sliced mushrooms
- 4 garlic cloves, minced
- 2 pounds lamb, cut up
- 2 tablespoons safflower oil
- 2 yams, peeled and cut into thick slices
- 3 turnips, peeled, and cut into 1-inch dice
- 5 tomatoes, quartered
- 4 large zucchini, sliced
- 2 cups chopped watercress
- 1 cup chopped celery
- 2 cups chopped parsley
- 2 tablespoons sugar
- 2 tablespoons salt
- 2 tablespoons dried tarragon
- 3 tablespoons butter
- 4 cups water
- 1 cup cornstarch (optional)
- pepper

Sauté onions, mushrooms, garlic and lamb in safflower oil. Combine all ingredients except water, cornstarch and pepper in a large pot. Add the 4 cups water and simmer over low heat for 1 hour, or longer if desired. Thicken with the cornstarch mixed with a little cold water. Heat for a few minutes, stirring to blend. Add pepper to taste.

Serves 10

COOKING AND PREP TIME: 1 hour, 10 minutes

TANGY HAM AND CORN

- 2 pounds cooked ham
- 2 cups fresh corn kernels
- 3 celery ribs, cut up
- ½ cup vinegar
- ½ cup soy sauce
- 1 tablespoon prepared mustard
- ½ cup water
- pepper

Cut ham into bite-size squares. Place ham, corn and celery in a colander. Set colander (a bowl will also work) in a wok. Pour vinegar, soy sauce and mustard into bottom of wok with ½ cup water. Cover and steam for 15 minutes. Add pepper to taste. Serve with green salad.

Serves 8

COOKING AND PREP TIME: 25 minutes

BEEF WITH PEAS AND PEANUTS

- 4 tablespoons safflower oil
- 1 cup unsalted raw peanuts
- 4 tablespoons cornstarch
- 5 tablespoons soy sauce
- 3 tablespoons dry sherry
- 1 pound lean beef, cut into short strips
- 1 cup sliced mushrooms
- 1 cup shelled fresh peas
- 1 cup chopped scallions
- 1 cup bean sprouts
- 1 teaspoon salt
- pepper

Heat 2 tablespoons of the oil in a wok until almost smoking. Stir-fry peanuts for 30 seconds. Cover and continue to cook over low heat for 1 minute. Remove peanuts and set aside in a covered dish. Combine 3 tablespoons of the cornstarch with soy sauce and sherry in a bowl. Add beef and mix. Reheat the oil in the wok (add more oil if needed) and stir-fry beef until it has browned. Remove beef and sauce and set aside. Add remaining oil to wok and stir-fry vegetables. Reduce heat, and combine all ingredients in the wok. Add the salt, and pepper to taste. Cover and heat for 3 minutes. May be served alone or with rice.

Serves 4

COOKING AND PREP TIME: 20 minutes

AIMLESS SWEET-AND-SOUR LAMB

Aimless, Annapolis

- 2 pounds lean lamb, cut in thin strips
- 2 pounds zucchini, sliced thin and quartered
- 1 sweet green pepper, seeded, cut in squares
- 2½ tablespoons sesame oil
- 2 cups sliced mushrooms
- 10 ounces water-packed artichoke hearts, drained
- salt and pepper
- Sweet-and-Sour Sauce (p. 118)

Heat oil in a wok, and stir-fry lamb strips for about 4 minutes. Push lamb out of oil and add vegetables. Stir-fry until vegetables are crisp-tender; take care not to overcook. Mix lamb with vegetables, and season with salt and pepper to taste. Serve with sweet-and-sour sauce.

Serves 4

COOKING AND PREP TIME: 15 minutes

STIR-FRY SQUID

- 2 pounds squid, cleaned, sliced in rings (remove skin if you like)
- 2 tablespoons olive oil
- 1 cup pitted black olives, cut up
- 3 garlic cloves, minced
- 1 cup cooked or canned baby lima beans
- 2 large ripe tomatoes, peeled and cut up
- ¼ cup sherry
- 1 tablespoon honey
- salt and pepper

Bring squid to a boil; drain. Heat oil in a wok. Stir-fry squid, olives, garlic and lima beans. Add tomatoes, sherry and honey. Stir thoroughly. Cover and simmer for 3 minutes. Add salt and pepper to taste. Serve very hot.

Serves 4

COOKING AND PREP TIME: 15 minutes

Just south of Halifax, one of hundred of rocky Nova Scotia inlets out of which sail the "finest kind" of fishing fleets in the world.

STEAMED FISH

- 2½ pounds fish fillets, any kind, cut into 5 portions
- 4 tomatoes, peeled and quartered
- 1 cup cut-up bamboo hearts
- 1 tablespoon butter
- 1 cup mild sauerkraut
- ¼ cup vinegar
- ¼ cup soy sauce
- ¼ cup white wine
- salt and pepper
- ¼ cup water

Place fish, tomatoes, bamboo hearts, butter and sauerkraut in a colander in the bottom of a wok. Pour in vinegar, soy sauce, wine and seasonings to taste with ¼ cup water. Cover and steam for 10 to 15 minutes. Serve with brown rice or salad.

Serves 5

COOKING AND PREP TIME: 20 minutes

KIELBASA

Windsong, Newport

- 1 pound kielbasa (Polish sausage), sliced diagonally
- 1 stalk of fresh anise, cut into 1-inch lengths
- 3 tablespoons butter
- 1½ cups thin slices of mushrooms
- 2 zucchini, shredded
- salt and pepper

Combine ingredients with salt and pepper to taste in a shallow oven-proof dish. Wrap dish in foil and place 6 to 8 inches above the coals. Let the ingredients steam in the butter for 25 minutes.

Serves 4

COOKING AND PREP TIME: 30 minutes

HARBOR BLUEFISH DINNER

Condor, Sebastian Inlet, Florida

"When I see fish jumping, I go after them."

- 1 bluefish, cleaned, but not filleted
- 1 red onion, sliced
- 2 tablespoons butter
- 1 tablespoon chili powder

Place fish on foil. Scatter onion slices in cavity and around the fish. Dot with butter and sprinkle with chili powder. Wrap in foil, and place in hibachi coals for 20 minutes.

Serves 6

COOKING AND PREP TIME: 35 minutes

STEWARD'S STUFFING

Schooner *Bill of Rights*, Newport

(for turkey, roasting chicken, small whole fryer, or fish)

- 2 large onions, cut up
- 4 garlic cloves, minced
- 4 tablespoons butter
- 1 cup water or broth
- 2½ cups garlic croutons or toasted garlic bread
- ½ pound sausage, cut up small
- 3 scallions, cut up
- 1 cup crushed almonds
- 1 cup crushed saltines
- ¼ cup sherry
- ½ teaspoon ground sage

Sauté onions and garlic in 1 tablespoon butter. Add 1 cup water or broth. Slowly stir in croutons until blended. Add remaining ingredients. Cover and cook, stirring often with a fork, for 10 minutes. If too moist, cook without a cover; if too dry, add more water or broth.

Makes approximately 4 cups

COOKING AND PREP TIME: 15 to 20 minutes

HIBACHI HAM AND PINEAPPLE

- 7 pounds ham, cut into long strips
- 4 tablespoons melted butter
- 1 fresh pineapple, peeled and cut up
- 4 tablespoons lime juice
- 3 tablespoons honey
- 2 tablespoons brown sugar
- 1 tablespoon dry mustard
- 1 teaspoon ground cloves
- ¼ teaspoon ground sage
- ½ cup water

Broil ham strips on the hibachi grill. Baste with butter while cooking. Combine remaining ingredients with ½ cup water in a pan, and cook on the hibachi, stirring often to blend. When ham is cooked, spoon on sauce and serve.

Serves 11

COOKING AND PREP TIME: 45 minutes

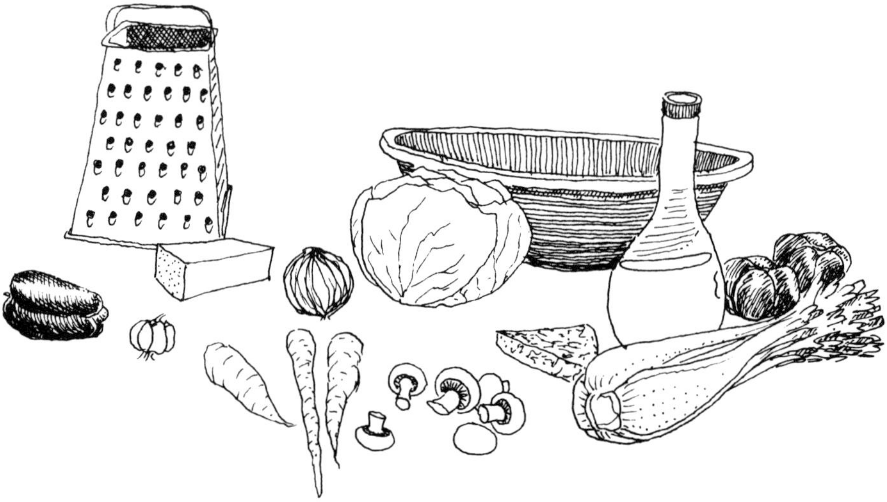

Chapter Twelve

VEGETABLES, SALADS AND SAUCES

FOIL-BAKED WHITE POTATOES

4 baking potatoes, scrubbed
¼ pound butter
½ cup snipped chives

Halve potatoes and puncture each half with a fork 3 or 4 times. Top each potato with some of the butter, and chives, and place in an ovenproof baking pan. Cover with foil, leaving an airspace. Heat directly over coals for 40 minutes.

Serves 4

COOKING AND PREP TIME: 50 minutes

FOIL-BAKED SWEET POTATOES

4 small sweet potatoes, peeled and cut into cubes
4 tablespoons brown sugar
2 tablespoons butter
1 teaspoon ground cinnamon

Place sweet potatoes in an ovenproof pan, and cover loosely with foil. Bake above coals for 15 minutes. Mix brown sugar, butter and cinnamon in a pan and place over low heat, stirring until blended. Lift foil and pour sauce over potatoes. Reseal foil and bake for another 15 to 20 minutes.

Serves 4

COOKING AND PREP TIME: 40 minutes

GREEN BEANS WITH PEANUT-BUTTER SAUCE

Cutter *Geraldine*, Morehead City, North Carolina

- 1 pound fresh green beans, cut into 1-inch lengths
- 3 tablespoons peanut butter
- 1 teaspoon honey
- 1 teaspoon soy sauce
- 1 teaspoon dry vermouth
- 1 teaspoon instant coffee powder
- 6 tablespoons water

Cook beans in water until tender but still crisp, about 10 minutes. Drain and set aside. While beans are cooking, combine remaining ingredients in a saucepan. Cook, stirring, over low heat until blended. Pour sauce over beans and serve. (The hot sauce is also excellent on top of many cold vegetables.)

Serves 5

COOKING AND PREP TIME: 20 minutes

PIGEON PEAS AND RICE

Jade Princess, Fresh Creek, Andros Island

- 2 cups uncooked brown rice
- 2½ cups canned pigeon peas
- 2 tablespoons butter
- ½ tablespoon oil
- 1 small onion, cut up
- 3 ounces tomato paste
- ½ teaspoon dried thyme
- ½ cup hot water
- salt and pepper

Cook rice in water until done to your taste. Drain pigeon peas and rinse with cold water. Melt butter in a skillet, and add oil. Add onion and saute until golden brown. Add pigeon peas and cook over low heat, stirring often, for 4 minutes. Add tomato paste, thyme and ½ cup hot water to make sauce. Stir while heating. Season to taste. Serve over rice.

Serves 4

COOKING AND PREP TIME: 15 minutes

CHICK-PEA SUCCOTASH

- 3 slices of salt pork, diced
- 1½ cups shelled fresh baby lima beans
- 1½ cups canned chick-peas, drained
- 3 tomatoes, cut up
- ½ teaspoon ground aniseed
- ¼ teaspoon dried marjoram
- 2 beef bouillon cubes
- 2 cups water
- salt and pepper

Combine ingredients in a pot, including the 2 cups water and salt and pepper to taste. Simmer, stirring occasionally, for 30 minutes. For variety, serve with grated cheese.

Serves 5

COOKING AND PREP TIME: 40 minutes

FOIL-BAKED ACORN SQUASH

- 3 acorn squash, halved and seeded
- 2 tablespoons butter
- 1 tablespoon ground cinnamon
- ½ lemon

Place a pat of butter in each squash half, along with a dash of cinnamon and a thin slice of lemon. Wrap each squash half in foil and bake among hibachi coals for 20 minutes.

Serves 6

COOKING AND PREP TIME: 25 minutes

CHEESE CELERY

- ½ pound ricotta cheese
- ½ teaspoon lemon juice
- ¼ teaspoon black pepper
- 3 celery ribs, cut into 3-inch lengths

Blend cheese, lemon juice and pepper with a fork. Stuff celery and serve. Excellent as an appetizer.

Serves 4

PREP TIME: 5 minutes

FOIL-BAKED ZUCCHINI

- 8 large zucchini, cut into halves lengthwise
- 6 ounces tomato paste
- 1½ tablespoons olive oil
- 1 teaspoon dried orégano
- salt and pepper
- ¼ pound any cheese, sliced long and thin

Make deep gashes all over top of zucchini halves. Place them in an ovenproof pan. Mix tomato paste, olive oil, orégano and seasoning to taste, and spread on top of halved zucchini. Top with cheese. Cover tightly with foil and bake over coals for 30 minutes.

Serves 8

COOKING AND PREP TIME: 40 minutes

CUCUMBER SALAD

- 2 cucumbers, sliced thin
- 1 tablespoon minced dill
- 2 tablespoons minced parsley
- 1 teaspoon dry mustard
- ¼ cup minced onion
- ¼ teaspoon pepper
- 1 teaspoon salt
- 1 teaspoon sugar
- 1 cup white vinegar

Combine ingredients in a covered dish and let stand for about 1 hour.

Serves 6

PREP TIME: 5 minutes plus as long as it sits

PEAS AND CARROT SALAD

- 4 carrots, shredded
- 1 cup shelled raw peas
- 1 cup shelled raw baby lima beans
- 2 ounces blue cheese, crumbled
- 1 tablespoon oil
- 1 tablespoon vinegar
- 1 teaspoon minced garlic
- salt and pepper

Put carrots, peas and lima beans in a bowl. Mix remaining ingredients, with salt and pepper to taste, into a dressing, blending well. Pour over vegetables and toss to blend. Let stand for at least 20 minutes before serving.

Serves 5

PREP TIME: 25 minutes

"JUST A SALAD"

Courtesan, West Islip, New York

- ½ head of cabbage, chopped
- 4 carrots, shredded
- 3 sweet green peppers, seeded, cut up small
- 2 tablespoons oil
- 1 tablespoon vinegar
- 1 tablespoon sugar
- 1 teaspoon whole aniseeds
- ½ teaspoon garlic salt
- ½ teaspoon salt
- ½ teaspoon black pepper

Put cabbage, carrots and peppers in a bowl. Blend other ingredients, stirring well; make sure to dissolve sugar. Pour over vegetables and toss.

Serves 6

PREP TIME: 5 to 10 minutes

BANANA-RAISIN SALAD

- 4 bananas, sliced thick
- 1½ cups sultana raisins
- ¼ to ½ cup brandy
- 3 tablespoons honey
- 2 tablespoons oil
- 2 tablespoons vinegar
- salt and pepper
- ¼ head of lettuce (large leaves are best)

Combine bananas, raisins, brandy to taste and honey. Blend oil, vinegar and seasoning to taste, and pour over banana mixture. Serve on top of lettuce.

Serves 5

PREP TIME: 5 minutes

HOT POTATO SALAD

8 medium-size boiling potatoes, peeled and cut up
¼ cup vinegar
1 tablespoon oil
1 tablespoon Worcestershire sauce
1 tablespoon red wine
4 scallions, chopped
1 teaspoon dry mustard
½ teaspoon salt
¼ teaspoon ground dill

Boil potatoes in water to cover until tender but not mushy. Meanwhile heat remaining ingredients in a saucepan, stirring occasionally. Drain potatoes and add the dressing. Cover and warm over very low heat for 5 minutes, or until thoroughly hot. Serve hot or cold.

Serves 6

COOKING AND PREP TIME: 35 minutes

BEAN-SPROUT AND EGG SALAD

3 hard-cooked eggs, sliced
2 cups bean sprouts
2 scallions, diced
1 cup sour cream (optional)
1 tablespoon oil
1 tablespoon vinegar
½ teaspoon black pepper
¼ teaspoon dry mustard

Arrange egg slices on a bed of bean sprouts and garnish with scallions. Mix remaining ingredients to make dressing, and pour over salad.

Serves 4

PREP TIME: 12 minutes

GARDEN SALAD

¼ head of lettuce, cut up
2 tomatoes, cut up
½ cucumber, sliced thin
juice of ½ lemon
2 tablespoons oil
½ tablespoon vinegar
½ teaspoon minced dill
salt

Combine vegetables, dressing ingredients, and salt to taste. Toss and serve.

Serves 4

PREP TIME: 5 minutes

BEANS, BEANS, BEANS

- ½ cup cooked green beans
- ½ cup cooked baby lima beans
- ½ cup canned kidney beans, drained
- ½ cup cooked lentils
- 3 scallions, diced
- 3 ounces sour cream
- 2 tablespoons safflower oil
- 2 tablespoons lemon juice
- 1 teaspoon minced chervil
- ¼ teaspoon pepper
- salt

Combine beans, lentils and scallions. Mix remaining ingredients, with salt to taste, to make dressing, and toss with beans. Let stand for 10 minutes, chilling if desired. Toss gently, and serve with lettuce or alone.

Serves 4

PREP TIME: 20 minutes

TEXAS SEAMAN'S SALAD

- 1 large avocado, peeled, cut up
- 1 cup cooked chick-peas, drained
- 1 cup pitted whole black olives
- 4 pimientos, quartered
- ½ cup shredded Cheddar cheese
- 2 tablespoons safflower oil
- 1 tablespoon lemon juice
- 1 tablespoon wine vinegar
- salt and pepper
- ½ pound spinach, washed, drained, torn into large pieces

With a fork, mash together vegetables (except spinach) and cheese. Add dressing ingredients and seasoning to taste. Serve the mixture in scoops on spinach leaves. Will also work on crackers as a snack.

Serves 4

PREP TIME: 10 minutes

Looking across the Potomac from the Yacht Basin.

CHICK-PEA SALAD

Legation, Washington, D.C.

2 cups cooked chick-peas
4 scallions, minced
¼ cup safflower oil
3 tablespoons chopped parsley
1 tablespoon vinegar
¼ teaspoon salt

Combine ingredients in a bowl and toss thoroughly.

Serves 4

PREP TIME: 3 minutes

SEA CHEF'S DRESSING*

- 5 tablespoons oil
- 4 tablespoons vinegar
- 1 tablespoon lemon juice
- 1 teaspoon garlic powder
- ½ teaspoon salt
- ½ teaspoon lemon pepper
- ¼ teaspoon dry mustard

Mix ingredients thoroughly.

Makes ⅓ cup

PREP TIME: 5 minutes

* HINT: Dressing may be premixed ashore to save time and space aboard.

SWEET-AND-SOUR SAUCE

Aimless, Annapolis, Maryland

A tangy, versatile sauce for meat, fish and vegetables.

- ½ cup brown sugar
- ½ cup vinegar
- 1 teaspoon dry mustard
- 3 tablespoons soy sauce
- 1 teaspoon lemon juice
- cornstarch mixed with cold water (optional)

Combine everything except cornstarch in a wok. Heat, stirring until blended. If sauce needs to be thickened, add a slurry of cornstarch mixed with cold water, and simmer until thickened. Serve.

Makes 1 cup

COOKING AND PREP TIME: 5 minutes

SPAGHETTI SAUCE

Schooner *Bill of Rights*, Newport

- 2 cups chopped onions
- 3 cups sliced mushrooms
- 2 tablespoons grated fresh gingerroot
- 2 garlic cloves, minced
- 2 tablespoons butter
- 3 beef bouillon cubes
- 3 cups hot water
- 5 tomatoes, chopped
- 6 tablespoons tomato paste
- 2 tablespoons oil
- 2 tablespoons dried orégano
- 2 tablespoons dried basil
- 2 bay leaves
- 1 teaspoon black pepper
- salt

Sauté onions, mushrooms, gingerroot and garlic in the butter in a 4-quart kettle for 5 minutes. Dissolve bouillon cubes in 3 cups hot water, and add to saucepan. Add tomatoes, tomato paste, oil, herbs and black pepper. Simmer, stirring occasionally, for 45 minutes. Add salt to taste.

Serves 6 to 8

COOKING AND PREP TIME: 1 hour

MUSHROOM SAUCE MOZAMBIQUE

- 3 cups sliced fresh mushrooms
- 1 lime, sliced thin
- 2 garlic cloves, sliced
- 2½ tablespoons butter
- ½ cup lime juice
- ¼ cup dry vermouth
- 1¼ tablespoons flour
- 1 cup milk
- salt and pepper

Sauté mushrooms, lime slices and garlic in 1 tablespoon of the butter for 3 minutes. Add lime juice and vermouth. Cover and keep warm over very low heat. Melt remaining 1½ tablespoons butter in a pan. Add flour, stirring until blended. Add milk and cook over medium heat, stirring until creamy, but do not boil. Add mushroom mixture. Stir to mix. Serve hot. Tasty addition to cold or hot meat or vegetables.

Serves 4

COOKING AND PREP TIME: 15 minutes

Chapter Thirteen
DESSERT

BUZZARDS BAY BLUEBERRIES

- 1 pint blueberries, washed and stemmed
- 1 tablespoon sugar
- ¼ cup chopped cashews or walnuts
- 1 banana, mashed
- ¾ cup heavy cream or milk

Mix sugar and nuts with mashed banana. Spoon over blueberries. Top with 2 tablespoons cream per serving, or use milk.

Serves 4

PREP TIME: 5 minutes

AUGMENTED APPLESAUCE

- 8 apples, peeled and cut up
- 2 bananas, peeled and mashed
- ½ cup raisins
- 1 tablespoon lemon or lime juice
- 1 tablespoon brown sugar
- 1 tablespoon ground cinnamon
- ¼ teaspoon grated nutmeg
- 1 cup water

Combine all ingredients in a pot with a snug cover. Simmer for 20 minutes, stirring often. Mash until ingredients are well blended. Serve hot or cold.

Serves 8

COOKING AND PREP TIME: 35 minutes

KUMQUATS AU RHUM

- 12 stewed or baked kumquats, halved and pitted
- 1 teaspoon lime juice
- ½ cup Jamaican rum

Macerate kumquats in lime juice and rum for 20 minutes. Serve them with the rum sauce.

Serves 3

PREP TIME: 25 minutes

GERMAN PEACH DESSERT

Segelschulschiff Gorch Fock, Kiel, West Germany

- 20 ounces canned peaches in syrup
- 1 cup German sauerkraut in wine
- ½ cup brandy

Chop the peaches. Combine ingredients, chill if possible, and serve.

Serves 4

PREP TIME: 5 minutes

BRANDY AND FRUIT

Courtesan, West Islip, New York

- 2 tablespoons brown sugar
- 1 tablespoon warm water
- 1 cup shredded coconut
- ½ cup brandy, warmed
- 4 fresh oranges, peeled and separated into sections

Dissolve sugar in 1 tablespoon warm water. Combine with coconut and brandy, and gently mix with orange sections.

Serves 5

COOKING AND PREP TIME: 5 minutes

KEY LEMON PIE

Aquarius, Key Largo, Florida

The British navigator and explorer, Captain James Cook, had to take the cat-o'-nine-tails in hand to induce his reluctant crew to eat scurvy-preventing citrus. This dish will be eagerly received without any such "enticements."

- 1 cup milk
- 1 teaspoon sugar
- 2 egg yolks
- ¼ cup lemon juice
- ¼ cup lime juice

Mix milk and sugar. Beat egg yolks with a fork until foamy. Combine milk, egg yolks and remaining ingredients. Pour into a prepared crust (graham-cracker crust works very well). Let cool in refrigerator for 50 minutes.

Serves 5

PREP TIME: 1 hour

RABBLE RAISINS

- 1 cup raisins
- 2 cups peeled orange slices
- 1½ cups shredded coconut
- ½ cup dry sherry

Combine ingredients and serve.

Serves 4

PREP TIME: 8 minutes

PINEAPPLE CARIBBEAN

Aquarius, Key Largo, Florida

- 1 pineapple, peeled and cut into cubes
- ½ cup Jamaican rum
- 3 tablespoons sugar

Combine pineapple with rum and sugar, and chill if possible.

Serves 5

PREP TIME: 5 minutes

HIBACHI APPLES

4 apples, cored
2 tablespoons brown sugar
3 tablespoons ground cinnamon
2 tablespoons butter

Remove peel from top quarter of each apple. Mix remaining ingredients with a fork until mostly blended. Place apples in foil and spoon butter mixture into apples. Wrap foil tightly around apples (each one wrapped individually works best) and place just above hibachi coals. Cook for about 20 minutes. This is also an excellent breakfast dish.

Serves 4

COOKING AND PREP TIME: 30 minutes

SWISS CHEESE FONDUE WITH BANANAS

4 bananas, cut into 1-inch sections
1 pound Swiss cheese, cut up
½ cup sherry
2 tablespoons jam
1 teaspoon grated nutmeg

Combine all ingredients except bananas in a fondue pot and heat until melted, stirring often to blend. When melted and hot, spread banana sections around the base of the fondue pot and serve. Dip banana sections into mixture to eat.

Serves 4

COOKING AND PREP TIME: 15 to 20 minutes

CHOCOLATE FRUIT FONDUE

Valkyrie, Rye, New York

1 pound milk chocolate
2 pears, cut into chunks
2 apples, cut into chunks
2 peaches, cut into quarters

Melt chocolate in a fondue pot. Dip fruit into chocolate to eat.

Serves 4

COOKING AND PREP TIME: 10 minutes

HONEY CANTALOUPE

1 ripe cantaloupe
½ cup sweet vermouth
½ cup almonds, ground
½ cup honey

Cut cantaloupe into halves, remove rind and seeds, and cut up into bite-size cubes. Combine vermouth, almonds and honey, and pour over melon pieces. Chill if possible.

Serves 5

PREP TIME: 10 minutes

Chapter Fourteen
FONDUE

Though a conventional fondue pot is easiest to use, a regular pot, heated by candle, Sterno, or a few coals in the hibachi, can serve the same purpose and save room. Additional fondue recipes can be found in the Dessert chapter.

SWISS CHEESE FONDUE

- 1 pound Swiss cheese, cut up
- ¼ pound ricotta cheese
- 2 teaspoons whole aniseeds
- 2 pounds raw vegetables, cut up
- 2 cups milk
- ½ cup soy sauce
- 3 tablespoons butter

Combine both cheeses, aniseeds, milk and soy sauce in a pot, and stir over low heat until blended and hot. Melt butter and add to pot. Dip vegetables into fondue.

Serves 6

COOKING AND PREP TIME: 20 minutes

MOZZARELLA FONDUE

- 1½ pounds mozzarella cheese, cut up
- ¼ pound blue cheese, crumbled
- 2 pounds raw vegetables, cut up
- 3 tablespoons butter
- ½ cup sherry
- salt and pepper

Combine cheeses, butter and sherry in a pot. Heat over very low heat. Stir slowly until cheese has melted and mixture is hot and blended. Add salt and pepper to taste. Arrange vegetables around pot. Dip vegetables into cheese to eat.

Serves 6

COOKING AND PREP TIME: 25 minutes

BEANS FONDUE

- 1 pound baked beans and pork, mashed
- 1 pound Cheddar cheese, cut up
- ½ cup dry vermouth
- 1 cup orange juice
- salt and pepper
- 8 slices of whole-wheat bread, cut into fork-sized pieces

Combine beans and cheese with vermouth and orange juice in a pot, and stir over low heat until melted, blended and hot. Add salt and pepper to taste. Cut the bread into pieces to fit on a fork. Dip bread into bean fondue.

Serves 6

COOKING AND PREP TIME: 20 minutes

FEARLESS FONDUE

Tiger, Melbourne, Florida

- 1 pound Cheddar cheese, shredded
- 3 ounces blue cheese, crumbled
- 1 cup sherry
- salt and pepper
- ½ loaf of rye bread, cut in small squares

Melt cheeses, stirring with a fork until smooth. Blend in sherry, and add salt and pepper to taste. Serve melted cheese in a pot over warming fire. Dip bread squares on long forks into cheese to eat.

Serves 5 or 6

COOKING AND PREP TIME: 15 minutes

Chapter Fifteen
SNACKS

JERKY

Make at home. This dish, a staple of the trappers who once explored the North American forests, is an ideal snack to feed the midnight watch.

- 2 pounds lean beef, cut into long, thick strips, an inch wide
- 1 teaspoon dry mustard
- ½ cup vinegar
- 1 teaspoon salt
- 1 teaspoon pepper
- ½ cup soy sauce

Marinate beef in mustard, vinegar, salt, pepper and soy sauce for 24 hours. Drain beef and dry with paper towels. Place on a wire rack in an oven heated to 150° F. for 24 hours. Jerky should have the consistency of tough leather.

PEMMICAN

This was once the survival food of explorers.

- 1 cup suet
- 1½ pounds jerky
- ½ cup pitted dates
- ½ cup raisins

Combine ingredients in a pan and place over low heat, stirring and mashing until blended. Jerky will become soft as lard heats around it. Let cool and cut into pieces.

COOKING AND PREP TIME: 30 minutes

GRANOLA

Make at home.

1 cup honey
2 cups wheat germ
1 cup cashews, chopped
1 cup shelled pecans, chopped
1 pound coconut meat, shredded
1 pound white raisins

Combine honey, wheat germ and nuts. Preheat oven to 300° F. Spread mixture on a baking pan and bake for 15 minutes. Combine with coconut and raisins.

COOKING AND PREP TIME: 25 minutes

Chapter Sixteen

MEALS FOR STORMY WEATHER

SEAFOOD STEW

- 2 pounds shellfish in shells
- 3 pounds fish, filleted
- 10 small white onions
- 1½ cups sherry
- 4 tomatoes, cut up
- 3 tablespoons honey
- 3 tablespoons dried orégano
- 3 basil leaves
- 3 tablespoons minced parsley
- 4 cups water
- salt and pepper

Put all ingredients except seasoning in a large pot with the 4 cups water. Cover and simmer for 25 minutes. Season to taste. Serve seafood with broth. Pasta may be added if desired.

Serves 5 (all day)

COOKING AND PREP TIME: 40 minutes

MUESLI

Bylgia, The Netherlands

- 1 orange
- 1 banana
- 1 cup wheat germ
- 1 cup raisins
- ½ cup oatmeal
- ¼ cup lemon juice

Peel and section orange. Peel banana and cut into thick slices. Combine all the ingredients, and serve with milk or juice.

Serves 4

PREP TIME: 3 minutes

Pulling boat to the *Grace B,* Jonesboro, Maine.

CAPTAIN LEIF'S CORNED BEEF

Fiddler's Green, Bar Harbor

3 pounds corned beef brisket, precooked ashore
3 pounds potatoes, halved
1 head of cabbage, quartered*
2 tablespoons butter
3 bay leaves
1 garlic clove, minced
salt and pepper

Place precooked beef in a pot and just barely cover with water. Cover the pot and simmer for 30 minutes. Add potatoes and cook for another 20 minutes. Add cabbage, butter, bay leaves and garlic. Cover, and simmer for at least 15 minutes more. May be kept hot all day. Season to taste when served.

Serves 5 (all day)

COOKING AND PREP TIME: 1 hour, 10 minutes

*HINT: By tasting a leaf of cabbage before you buy, you can select a mild one, which is better for cooking with corned beef.

STEWED TOMATOES

There's something about stewed tomatoes that once made them the first food cowpunchers sought after months on dusty trails. That something was the high vitamin C content of tomatoes.

Courtesan, West Islip, New York

- 2 large onions, cut up
- 2 tablespoons butter
- 10 tomatoes, cut in chunks
- 3 slices of rye toast, cubed
- 2 cups cut-up celery
- 1½ tablespoons salt
- 1 tablespoon black pepper
- 1 tablespoon garlic salt

Sauté onions in butter. Add remaining ingredients and bring to a boil. Reduce heat and simmer, covered, for 20 minutes.

Serves 5

COOKING AND PREP TIME: 30 minutes

CAPE FEAR KIDNEY BEAN STEW

Shrimpdragger *Joan,* Wilmington, North Carolina

Feel free to experiment with this one. The striker who gave it to me said he never made it the same way twice.

- 4 sweet potatoes, sliced thin
- 3 onions, quartered and separated
- 1 pound zucchini, cut up
- 1 pound cooked ham, chopped
- ¼ pound sausage, chopped
- ¼ cup diced salt pork
- 1½ quarts cooked kidney beans
- 1 teaspoon dried thyme
- ½ teaspoon dry mustard
- salt and pepper

Combine ingredients except seasoning in a large pot. Cover with water and cook over medium heat about 40 minutes. May be kept hot or reheated as needed. Season to taste when served.

Serves 4 (all day)

COOKING AND PREP TIME: 50 minutes

SAILOR'S STEW

- 1 pound beef, cut into cubes
- 1 head of cabbage, shredded
- 3 large tomatoes, cut up
- 2 large onions, chopped
- 2 garlic cloves, minced
- 3 pears, cored, cut up
- 4 cups sauerkraut
- 2 cups sliced mushrooms
- 3 tablespoons butter
- 1 cup red wine
- 2 tablespoons brown sugar
- 1 bay leaf
- 1 teaspoon black pepper
- 2 cups water
- salt

Combine ingredients including 2 cups water in a large pot. Bring to a boil, then reduce heat and simmer, covered, for 1 hour. Add salt to taste.

Serves 5 (all day)

COOKING AND PREP TIME: 1 hour, 10 minutes

FISH STEW

C-Away, Hatchet Bay, North Eleuthera Island

- 2 pounds fish, cleaned
- 6 potatoes, peeled and cut up
- 3 tomatoes, cut up
- 3 cups any vegetables
- ½ cup dry vermouth (adds some zip)
- 1 teaspoon red cayenne (adds more zip)
- 1 teaspoon grated nutmeg
- 1 bay leaf
- salt and pepper
- 1 cup water

Combine ingredients with seasoning to taste in a pot with 1 cup water. Simmer for 25 minutes or longer, adding more water if necessary.

Serves 5

COOKING AND PREP TIME: 35 minutes

Nightfall off Goat Island, Rhode Island. The Narragansett Bay Bridge spans the background.

BEAN SOUP

- 1 cup kidney beans
- 1 cup navy beans
- 1 cup lentils
- 3 large zucchini, cut up
- 4 celery ribs, cut up
- 4 tomatoes, cut up
- 1 lemon, sliced thin
- 2 cups uncooked brown rice
- 1 cup sherry
- ½ cup soy sauce
- 3 bouillon cubes
- 1 teaspoon dried thyme
- ½ teaspoon ground aniseed
- 6 cups water

If beans and lentils are not canned or cooked, presoak them overnight. Combine ingredients in a large pot with 6 cups water. Cover and bring to a boil. Simmer for 45 minutes, or until rice and beans are done. Season to taste when served.

Serves 5 (all day)

COOKING AND PREP TIME: 50 minutes

MINESTRONE SOUP

- ½ pound mild sausage, sliced thin
- 2 garlic cloves, minced
- 2 large onions, chopped
- ½ head of fresh fennel, chopped
- 3 yellow squash, cut up
- 2 sweet green peppers, seeded, cut up
- 2 tablespoons safflower oil
- 2 tablespoons butter
- 2 cups cooked lentils
- 3 vegetable bouillon cubes
- 1 bay leaf
- ½ teaspoon dried thyme
- 4 cups water

Sauté sausage, garlic and onions in oil and butter. Combine with remaining ingredients including 4 cups water in a large pot. Cover and bring to a boil. Reduce heat and simmer for 20 minutes.

Serves 4

COOKING AND PREP TIME: 40 minutes

Appendix

A TABLE OF SUBSTITUTIONS

1 tablespoon fresh herbs
½ tablespoon dried herbs

1 ounce cooking chocolate
3 tablespoons cocoa, plus 1 tablespoon fat

1 cup granulated white sugar
1 cup well-packed brown sugar
2 cups corn syrup and reduce liquid in recipe
¾ cup honey and reduce liquid in recipe
1½ cups maple syrup and reduce liquid in recipe
1½ cups molasses and reduce liquid in recipe
1½ cups sorghum and reduce liquid in recipe

1 cup all-purpose white flour
1 cup unbleached white flour
1 cup rye flour
1 cup whole wheat flour
⅓ cup soybean flour plus ⅔ cup all-purpose flour
1 cup and 2 tablespoons cake flour
⅞ cup rice flour
1 cup cornmeal

1 cup white rice
1 cup brown rice and allow more liquid and longer cooking time

1 cup butter

⅞ cup corn or peanut oil

1 cup margarine

⅞ cup lard plus 1 teaspoon salt (Lard cannot invariably be substituted for other fats since its fat content differs somewhat. For frying, etc., it won't cause any problems.)

1 cup fresh milk

½ cup evaporated milk plus ½ cup water

¼ cup dry milk solids plus ¾ cup water

½ cup condensed milk plus ½ cup water and less sugar than the recipe calls for

To make 1 cup sour milk add 1 tablespoon vinegar or lemon juice to enough milk so that together they make 1 cup of liquid; allow to stand for 5 minutes.

1 teaspoon baking powder (tartrate or phosphate)

⅔ teaspoon double-action baking powder

¼ teaspoon baking soda plus ½ teaspoon cream of tartar

¼ teaspoon baking soda plus ⅓ cup molasses

1 tablespoon flour (as a thickener)

½ tablespoon cornstarch

2 teaspoons quick-cooking tapioca

½ tablespoon potato flour

½ tablespoon barley flour

½ tablespoon arrowroot

INDEX

Acorn squash, foil-baked, 111
Aft galleys, 10
Aimless sweet-and-sour lamb, 103
Alcohol stoves, 15–16
Alcoholic beverages, 41–44
Apples, hibachi, 124
Applesauce, augmented, 121
Augmented applesauce, 121
Avocado Acapulco, 81

Baking powder, substitutions for, 142
Banana-raisin salad, 113
Bananas
  raisins and, salad, 113
  Swiss cheese fondue with, 124
Bass, 98
Bean soup, 138
Beans, beans, beans, 111
Beans fondue, 128
Bean-sprout and egg salad, 114
Bean-sprout sandwich, 79
Bean-sprouts
  salad, with egg, 114
  sandwiches, 79
  with egg, 78
Beans
  fondue, 128
  navy, 96
  salad, 115
  soup, 138
  stew, 136
Beef
  chipped, creamed, 65
  with peas and peanuts, 102
Beef with peas and peanuts, 102
Beer, 43
Beverages, 47
  alcoholic, 41–44
Blue breakfast, 67
Blueberries, 121
Bluefish, 98
  for breakfast, 67
  harbor dinner, 106
Blues, bass or flounder fry, 98
Boiled potatoes augmented, 82
Brandy and fruit, 122
Breakfast during winter in the Gulf, 66
Buckwheat cakes, 72
Butter, substitutions for, 142
Buzzards Bay blueberries, 121

Calamares, 95
Canned goods, 50–51
Cantaloupe, honey, 125
Cape Fear kidney bean stew, 136
Captain Leif's corned beef, 134–35
Carrots, salad of peas and, 112
Casserole, green bean, 84

Celery
  cheese, 111
  steamed, with fish, 93
Chapati, 89
Cheese
  celery stuffed with, 111
  fondue
    Fearless, 128
    mozzarella, 128
    Swiss, 124, 127
  "grill," 69
  storage of, 51
  vegetable omelet with, 70
Cheese celery, 111
Cheese "grill," 68
Cheese and vegetable omelet, 70
Chef's salad, 77
Chick-pea salad, 116
Chick-pea succotash, 111
Chick-peas
  salad, 116
  succotash, 111
Chicken
  oriental, 85
  in a pot, 96
Chicken in a pot, 96
China dinnerware, 23
Chipped beef, creamed, 65
Chive mussels, 100
Chocolate
  cooking, substitutions for, 141
  fondue with fruit, 124
Chocolate fruit fondue, 124
Clams, steamed, 93
Cleaning up, 24–25
Coal stoves, 14
Cold storage, 27–31
Corn and ham, tangy, 102
Corned beef, 134–35
Courtesan's creamed vegetables, 79
Creamed chipped beef, 65
Creamed vegetables, 79
Cucumber salad, 112
Curried morning mushrooms, 64
Curry, garden, 99

Deck hand's special, 72–73
Diesel oil stoves, 14–15
Dirtproofing of galley, 24–25
Dressing for salad, 117
Dried foods, storage of, 52
Drinking water, 58
Dual-fuel stoves, 16–17

Egg and tomato, 85
Eggs, 50
  panman egg stretcher, 69
  riced, 63
  salad, with beansprouts, 114
  sandwiches, with beansprouts, 78
  scrambled, and mussels, 67
  tomatoes and, 85
  with vegetables, 71
  See also Omelets
Eggstables, 71
Electric refrigerators, 31
Electric stoves, 16
Erbseneintopf, 92

Fearless fondue, 128
Fire extinguishers, 39
First aid kits, 59
Fish
  steamed, 104
    with celery, 93
  stew, 137
  See also specific types of fish
Fish stew, 137
Flashlights, 38–39
Flounder, 98
Flour, white, substitutions for, 141, 142
Foil-baked acorn squash, 111
Foil-baked sweet potatoes, 109
Foil-baked white potatoes, 109
Foil-baked zucchini, 112
Fondue
  beans, 128
  chocolate, with fruit, 124
  Fearless, 128
  mozzarella, 128
  Swiss cheese, 127
    with bananas, 124
Foul weather, food for, 39–40

French toast, 71
Fresh foods, 5
Fresh mussel meal, 100
Fruit, 46
  brandy and, 122
  chocolate fondue with, 124
  storage of, 51
  See also specific types of fruit
Fuels for stoves, 14–17

Galley, 9–25
  basic components of, 12–14
  cleaning of, 24–25
  location of, 10–11
  storage space in, 17–18
Garden curry, 99
Garden salad, 114
Gas stoves, 16
German peach dessert, 122
Granola, 132
Green bean "casserole", 84
Green beans with peanut-butter sauce, 110
Green beans
  in casserole, 84
  with peanut-butter sauce, 110
Grouper, 97

Ham
  corn and, 102
  pineapple and, 107
  sandwich, 75
Harbor bluefish dinner, 106
Herbs, substitutions for, 141
Hibachi apples, 124
Hibachi ham and pineapple, 107
Hibachis, 19–20
  apples cooked on, 124
  ham and pineapple cooked on, 107
  safety precautions for, 58
Honey cantaloupe, 125
Hot potato salad, 114

Ice, 30
Iceboxes, 28–29
  storing food in, 30–31

Jerky, 131
Jury-rigging, 33–36
"Just a salad", 113

Kapucijners, 84
Karl's delight, 80
Kerosene stoves, 14
Key lemon pie, 123
Kidney bean stew, 136
Kielbasa, 105
Knives, safety precautions for, 56–57
Kumquats au rhum, 122

Labskaus, 90
Lamb
  stew, 101
  sweet-and-sour, 103
Lemon pie, 123
Lentil burgers, 76
Liquid fuels for stoves, 14–16
Liquor, 42–43
  for cooking, 43–44
Lotus leaf cookery, 20–22

Meat
  potatoes and, 98
  storage of, 52
Meat and potatoes plus, 98
Metal serving gear, 24
Midship galleys, 10–11
Milk, substitutions for, 142
Minestrone soup, 139
Molasses ham sandwiches, 75
Mozzarella fondue, 128
Muesli, 133
Mushroom sauce Mozambique, 119
Mushrooms
  curried, 64
  sauce Mozambique, 119
Mussels
  chive, 100
  fresh, 100–1
  scrambled eggs with, 67
  spaghetti with, 97

Navy beans, 96
Navy beans civilian style, 96
Nogo Bay vegetables, 92

Oatmeal, 66
Omelets
  cheese and vegetable, 70
  One-eye-open, 65
One-eye-open omelet, 65
Oriental chicken, 85
Ovens, stove-top, 19
Oysters, 99
Oysters Delmarva, 99

Pancake sandwich, 77
Pancakes
  sandwich, 77
  spinach, 70
Pancakes Popeye, 70
Panman cakes, 63
Panman egg stretcher, 69
Pans, 22
Paper plates, 23–24
Pea soup thick as a fog, 81
Peaches, German, 122
Peanut-butter sauce, green beans with, 110
Peas
  beef with, 102
  carrots and, salad, 112
  soup, 81
Peas and carrot salad, 112
Pemmican, 131
Pie, Key lemon, 123
Pigeon peas and rice, 110
Pilaf, rice, 94
Pineapple
  Caribbean, 123
  ham and, 107
Pineapple Caribbean, 123
Plastic dinnerware, 23
Potatoes
  boiled, 82
  foil-baked, 109
  meat and, 98
  salad, hot, 114
Potholders, 38
Pots, 22
Prepackaged meals, 5
Propane stoves, 16
Protein sources, 46–47
Provisioning, 45–53
  for emergencies, 58
  planning for, 47–50
  storage and, 50–53

Rabble raisins, 123
Rarerarebit, 72
Refrigerators, 31
Rhode Island lamb stew, 101
Rice
  eggs and, 63
  pigeon peas and, 110
  pilaf, 94
  white, substitutions for, 141
Rice pilaf, 94
Riced eggs, 63

Safety precautions, 55–60
Sailor's stew, 137
Sailor's vegetable sukiyaki, 87
Salad
  banana and raisin, 113
  bean, 115
  beansprout and egg, 114
  chef's, 77
  chick-pea, 116
  cucumber, 112
  dressing for, 117
  garden, 114
  peas and carrot, 112
  potato, hot, 114
  sea chef's, 76
  steward's, 75
  Texas seaman's, 115
Salami, storage of, 51
Salmon stir fry, 86
Salsifying breakfast, 64
Sandwiches
  beansprout, 79
    with egg, 78
  molasses ham, 75
  pancake, 77
Sardines, stir-fried, 86
Sauces
  mushroom, 119
  spaghetti, 118
  sweet-and-sour, 118
Savory zucchini, 82

Scrambled eggs and mussels, 67
Sea bass, 97
Sea bass or grouper, 97
Sea chef's dressing, 117
Sea chef's salad number one, 76
Seafood stew, 133
Serving gear, 23
Single-pot stoves, 18–19
Sinks, 12–13
Solid fuels for stoves, 14
Soup
  bean, 138
  minestrone, 139
  pea, 81
Spaghetti
  with mussels, 97
  sauce for, 118
    thick, 80
Spaghetti with mussels, 97
Spaghetti sauce, 118
Spices, storage of, 52
Spinach pancakes, 70
Squash
  acorn, 111
  See also Zucchini
Squid, 95
  stir-fry, 103
Steamed celery and fish, 93
Steamed clams, 93
Steamed fish, 104
  with celery, 93
Sterno, 14, 18
Stew
  fish, 137
  kidney bean, 136
  sailor's, 137
  seafood, 133
Steward's salad, 75
Steward's stuffing, 106
Stewed tomatoes, 136
Stir-fried salmon, 86
Stir-fried sardines, 86
Stir-fry squid, 103
Storage, 17–18, 50–53
Stoves, 13–14
  fuels for, 14–17
  safety precautions for, 57–58
Stroganoff shazaam, 90
Stormy weather, cooking during, 37–40
Stuffing, 106
Succotash, chick-pea, 111
Sugar, white, substitutions for, 141
Sukiyaki, vegetable, 87
Sweet potatoes, foil-baked, 109
Sweet-and-sour lamb, 103
Sweet-and-sour sauce, 118
Sweets, 47
Swiss cheese fondue, 127
Swiss cheese fondue with bananas, 124

Tangy ham and corn, 102
Texas seaman's salad, 115
Thin spaghetti with thick sauce, 80
Toasters, 19
Tomatoes
  eggs and, 85
  stewed, 136

Utensils, 24

Vegetables, 46
  cheese omelet with, 70
  creamed, 79
  Nogo Bay, 92
  storage of, 51
  sukiyaki, 87
  See also specific vegetables

Windsong's egg and bean-sprout sandwich, 78
Wine, 41–42
Winter in Gulf breakfast, 66
Woks, 20–22
Wood stoves, 14

Zucchini
  foil-baked, 112
  savory, 82